Nancy Astor

Nancy Astor

A Lady Unashamed

JOHN GRIGG

Little, Brown and Company
BOSTON

FIRST AMERICAN EDITION
LIBRARY OF CONGRESS CATALOG CARD NUMBER
80-85094

Picture research by Emily Astor
Designed by James Campus

Frontispiece: John Singer Sargent's portrait of Lady Astor at Cliveden
(courtesy, The National Trust)

PRINTED IN THE UNITED STATES OF AMERICA

*To
my mother*

Contents

Acknowledgements

❧

My greatest debt is to the Hon. David Astor for his most generous and wide-ranging help. Apart from all the direct assistance he has given me, he has been the medium through which much additional help has come my way. To him and to his wife, Bridget, no thanks could be adequate.

I am also very deeply grateful to other members of the family – to the late Hon. Michael Astor, for his sage advice on many matters and for allowing me to quote remarks of his, as well as passages from his outstanding book, *Tribal Feeling*; to the Hon. Sir John Astor, for the stimulus of his comments and for allowing me to quote some of them; to him and to Sir Edward Ford, holders of the Nancy Astor copyright, for permission to quote copyright material, including Nancy's unpublished fragment of autobiography; to Mrs C.G. Lancaster, for her vivid recollections and opinions, and for allowing me to reproduce her portrait of Irene Gibson, by Dana Gibson; to the Hon. Mrs Reginald Winn, more especially for permission to quote from her fine book, *Always a Virginian* (published so far only in America), and to the Hon. Reginald Winn; to the Hon. Lady Ford, for most kindly allowing me to read and make use of the remarkable early letters written by her aunt to her mother; to the late Joyce Grenfell, some of whose words I have quoted, and to Mr Reginald Grenfell; to Viscount Astor, for his generosity in putting family photograph albums and the Cliveden visitors' books at my disposal, and for letting me reproduce one of his Sargent drawings of Nancy as the book's front cover; to the Hon. Emily Astor, for her enthusiastic help in choosing and searching for illustrations; to the Earl of Ancaster, the Hon. Mrs Christopher Bridge, Miss Elizabeth Winn and the Hon. Mrs Mark Wyndham.

Among many others who have helped me in various ways, I should like to express special gratitude to: Lady Altrincham, Miss Pat Burge, Marquesa Casa Maury, Mrs Leslie Cheek, the Hon. William Douglas-Home, Mrs Phyllis Draper, Dr J.A. Edwards (Archivist at Reading University and custodian of the Astor archive there), Mr Verne A. Ferguson, Mr Alastair Forbes, Mr Frank Goodey, Miss Margaret Jones, Miss Joyce Knight, Mr Freddie Knox, Mr and Mrs Edwin Lee, the

Acknowledgements

Earl of Longford (who, among other things, asked me to write the book), the Revd Douglas Pitt, Mrs M.C. Sleeman and (last only alphabetically) my wife.

Much as I owe to all who have helped me, I should emphasize that responsibility for all views and judgements put forward in the book – apart from those specifically attributed – is mine and mine alone.

Some of the material in the book was gathered while I was making a television documentary on Nancy, which was shown on BBC 2 in November 1979, and I wish to record my thanks to the BBC, more especially to the pro-gramme's very able producer, Mr Jeremy Bennett.

To Miss Jean Walton, who typed the book at her usual high speed, and to Miss Margaret Willes, who edited it with scrupulous care, I am more grateful than I can say.

J.G.

Publisher's Acknowledgements

We should like to thank the following for permission to reproduce pictures which they own or control: on page 14 (above), Verne A. Ferguson; on page 15, the late Joyce Grenfell; on page 34, by kind permission of the Directors of Baring Brothers & Co. Limited; on pages 89 and 113, Radio Times Hulton Picture Library; on pages 104 and 105, Edwin Lee; on page 106, Rosina Harrison; on page 129, Michael Tree; on page 131, Hon. Mrs Christopher Bridge; on pages 150 and 186, Emily Astor; on page 170, Jane Bown; on page 182, Lord Ancaster; and on page 185, the National Trust.

We should also like to thank the following publishers for permission to reproduce copyright material: Allen & Unwin for *Rhodesia That was My Life* (1968) by Robert Tredgold; and Jonathan Cape for the *Life of Noël Coward* (1976) by Cole Lesley.

[11]

1

American Prelude

❧

THE most loyal citizen of Danville, Virginia, would hardly describe it as a glamorous place. But it was the birthplace of two outstandingly glamorous women. Since about ten years ago this fact has been commemorated by a sign, rather like a miniature English pub sign, at the intersection of Main Street and Broad. On one side is written:

The Gibson Girl

Here stood the residence in which Irene Langhorne Gibson, 1873–1956, was born. Her beauty, charm and vivacity captivated the artist, Charles Dana Gibson, who, following their marriage in 1895, cast his celebrated, style-setting 'Gibson Girl' illustrations in her image.

The other side bears this inscription:

Lady Astor

Here stood the residence in which Nancy Langhorne, Viscountess Astor, 1879–1964, was born. Lady Astor, noted for her wit, advocacy of women's rights, strong views on temperance, and articulate affection for her native state, was the first woman to sit, 1919–1945, in the British House of Commons.

Apart from producing one of the first modern sex symbols and the first British woman MP, Danville has little to boast of historically. Only a medium-sized town even today, it has kept itself going on tobacco and textiles – industries whose background is well illustrated in the local museum – but it has seldom come to the notice of the world at large. In 1903, however, it was the scene of a sensational rail disaster, and earlier it had a moment of rather pathetic glory when it served as Jefferson Davis's capital during the last days of the Confederacy.

The American Civil War was a very recent and painful memory when Nancy Astor was a child. Her father, Chiswell Dabney Langhorne, was a young soldier in the Confederate Army at the time of his marriage to Nannie Witcher Keene. He was twenty-one; she was only seventeen. After the war they lived for twenty years

Nancy aged six or seven – just after the family moved from Danville to Richmond

in Danville, and ten of their eleven children were born there. Three died in infancy, but the survivors, in order of age, were Keene, Elizabeth (Lizzie), Irene, Harry, Nancy, Phyllis, William (known as Buck) and Nora (who alone was born after the family moved to Richmond in 1885).

Nancy was named after her mother, Nannie Witcher. It is under those names that her birth is registered in the records of the Danville Circuit Court and the date is given as 17 May 1879 – not 19 May, which became the accepted date of her birth. The friends and relations of her childhood always knew her as Nannie and it is not at all clear when or why her name was changed to Nancy. Probably the change was in some way connected with the family's much improved social circumstances when she was in her teens.

There was nothing remotely grand about the home in which she spent her first six years. The Langhornes' single-storey house on what was then the edge of Danville consisted of only four small rooms and a kitchen. (It is still there, though it has been moved a few yards to make way for an apartment block and a top storey has been added to it.) Colonel and Mrs Langhorne had any amount of Southern pride, but very limited resources when their children were small. The

Nancy's mother, Nannie Witcher Langhorne

[15]

OPPOSITE ABOVE *Birthplace at Danville (with top storey added)*
BELOW *Nancy's father, Chiswell Dabney Langhorne (right) with friend, at Mirador*

future mistress of Cliveden needed no imagination to be aware what it was like to be poor and to live in cramped conditions.

Her father's family, the Langhornes, had been established in Virginia since the late seventeenth century and there were Langhornes in Virginian politics before as well as after the American Revolution. But Chiswell Dabney Langhorne seems to have belonged to a relatively obscure branch of the family, though his maternal grandparents, the Dabneys, had a plantation near Lynchburg on which he spent much of his youth. On her mother's side Nancy had Irish blood – the Keenes are reputed to have come originally from County Donegal – and her mother's father was political in the rather minor sense that he was a state senator. In the fragment of autobiography that she produced towards the end of her life, Nancy remarks that, when she was young, 'people talked a lot about where they had come from and their ancestors'. For instance, the Dabneys were said to be descended from the Daubignys who invaded England with William the Conqueror. Her own attitude towards such matters was never one of total indifference. All the same, we should accept her statement that she was never very interested in where she came from; only in where she was going.

It is certainly wrong to suggest that her home background was sophisticated or refined. Her father may or may not have had patrician antecedents, but his own character was nearer to that of Squire Western than any contemporary English gentleman or aristocrat. Even when he became rich he did not cease to be the hot-tempered, rough-mannered, hard-drinking, self-willed man that he had always been. Habitually a chewer and spitter of tobacco, he asserted his right to spit even during church services; and one old coloured woman, who knew how choleric he could be, is reported to have said, 'If Mr Langhorne gits to heaven with all that cussing, there's hope for all us other sinners.' Yet he also had courage, humour, loyalty and notable powers of leadership. He was a man nobody could ignore, with the virtues and defects of the self-made rather than of one born to privilege. Whatever he may have lacked in culture, he had a fundamentally good heart, so that he was capable of both giving and inspiring the warmest affection. In his own rather primitive, patriarchal way he was utterly devoted to his wife and children, and he liked to be hospitable not only to friends but even to casual passers-by. From his first name, Chiswell, he had the nickname Chillie, which was pronounced Shillie; but his children normally addressed him as 'Sir'.

Nancy's mother had a temperament that was quite as strong as his, but with far more gentleness and sensitivity. She was a beauty – small, fair and with large blue eyes. She was also artistic. Without having ever been taught to read music she could play the piano and without having ever attended an art class she could paint in watercolour. She was a good needlewoman and a lover of flowers, who enjoyed working in a garden if ever she had the time. But most of her life was spent in child-bearing, child-rearing and ministering to her husband's needs. Her first grandchild was born before she herself had given birth to the last of her own children, Nora.

Alice Winn, a daughter of Lizzie, the eldest of the Langhorne girls, has written that from Mrs Langhorne (whom she called Nanaire)

came the famed beauty of her daughters, their love of gardens, their intense interest in people and their concern for those less fortunate than themselves, a sense of the ridiculous and a basic simplicity: [whereas from Chillie they inherited] the vitality and toughness that could be both bravery and tactlessness, the desire and talents to make a party go, and no self-consciousness.

Nancy has written thus of her parents:

People who knew my mother [in her young days] said that she was very pretty with a beautiful figure, but her great charm was her gaiety and her goodness. I daresay goodness and gaiety were not found together any more then than they are now. One way and another she must have had quite a time with Father. He adored her, and he never looked at another woman, but he had an ungovernable temper, and the common male weakness of expecting one dollar to do the work of two. I don't think he ever gave her quite enough money to run the large family on, even when the days came that he had plenty. But he was an amusing person, with great charm and courage and integrity, and everybody liked him. He never told the same story twice.

This and other passages in her memoir make us feel that she loved her mother more than her father, and so she probably did. Yet in personality she owed more to him. Ironically, it was Chillie's ambitious spirit that made her resent the male ascendancy that he himself so strongly typified.

Richmond, Virginia, devastated by the Civil War, showing (centre) the State Capitol, designed by Thomas Jefferson on the model of the Maison Carrée *at Nîmes*

A lesser man would have gone under, and his family with him, during the notorious years of 'Reconstruction' immediately after the Civil War. The South was a disaster area, ruined and ravaged. Work was exceedingly hard to come by, and at first Chillie had to scrape a living in a variety of more or less menial jobs. But after a time he established himself as an auctioneer, above all selling tobacco. His gift of the gab enabled him to develop an auctioneer's patter which was widely admired. Even so, life in Danville remained hard and precarious for the Langhornes. Looking back on her early childhood Nancy must have felt like Fanny Price in Jane Austen's *Mansfield Park*, contemplating the squalor of her parents' life in Portsmouth. A determination never again to be so restricted was clearly one of the driving forces of her career. She might occasionally express a preference for the simple life, but only from the vantage-point of colossal and secure wealth.

Even after Chillie decided to move to the state capital, Richmond, when Nancy was six years old, it was still several years before he got the lucky break which liberated the family from the nagging threat of destitution. Indeed, at the very moment when his luck turned he was at a particularly low ebb. But after his meeting in 1890 with Colonel Henry Douglas, an old friend who had obtained a contract for work on the Chesapeake and Ohio Railroad, Chillie was never again in financial difficulty. Though he had no qualifications for work on the engineering side, he claimed to be able to 'manage men and horses', and it was through his talents as a manager that he made his fortune in railroads.

In 1892 he bought a country estate near Charlottesville, at the same time retaining a house in Richmond, where Nancy was still going to school. The institution that she attended there was a school founded, owned and run by a remarkable woman, Virginia Randolph Ellett, who has to be regarded as one of the key figures in her life. Miss Jennie (as Miss Ellett was called) has been vividly described to the author by one of the last of her pupils, Mrs Leslie Cheek. She was small and bow-legged, always wore spats and walked very quickly. She had crinkled, gleaming eyes and a wonderful smile. But the most important thing about her was her passion for England. She did not teach her pupils American history, but she did make them learn the dates of the English kings, and even long passages from Burke's speech 'On Conciliation with the Colonies'. Learning by heart was, in her method of teaching, an essential discipline (as it should be in any well run school). Her pupils were drilled in Shakespeare and other great English authors. They had to give recitations and even talks in class. She arranged for the school's English competition to be judged by a Harvard professor who was a friend of hers. In fact she was in love with him and used to go to Harvard every summer, though Mrs Cheek doubts that her love was reciprocated.

Nancy claims, rather extravagantly, that Miss Jennie gave her a 'thirst for knowledge', a 'real liking for learning' and a 'passion for reading' that lasted the rest of her life. It would be truer to say that she acquired from Miss Jennie a lifelong respect for scholarly people, a taste for English literature that lasted until middle age and a permanent adroitness in the use of words. To her natural eloquence was added a sense of style, which enabled her to produce epigrams as well as wisecracks. Mrs Cheek recalls an exchange which shows how good Miss Jennie was at correcting verbal sloppiness. When she (Mrs Cheek) wrote in an essay or story that 'the sun sank like a great ball of fire', Miss Jennie was quick to point out that the simile was absurd because the sun *was* a great ball of fire. Nancy, too, must have benefited from such corrections. When she became a brilliant figure in the English establishment, Miss Jennie's joy and pride knew no bounds. She felt that Lady Astor MP was the supreme creation of her life, and Nancy in return – when she heard that Miss Jennie had no car – sent her a Model T Ford and also paid for a chauffeur. When Nancy visited the school, in its later years, a holiday was declared and all the girls were lined up to welcome her, holding chrysanthemums.

Despite Miss Jennie's influence, there was never any question of Nancy becoming a blue-stocking. She was a very intelligent woman, but her intelligence was always more intuitive than cerebral. She had no capacity for organizing her

Nancy's teacher, Virginia Ellett, 'Miss Jennie'

thoughts, and her critical faculties, though in some ways very acute, were in other ways surprisingly limited.

The Richmond of her childhood was recovering from the devastation of the Civil War, of which there were still many visible reminders. But in America what is not destroyed by conflict is more than likely to be destroyed by the relentless urge to modernize, and all the buildings in Richmond that were associated with Nancy have gone with the wind of change. The houses that the Langhorne family occupied – in Main Street, Third Street and Grace Street – have all disappeared, and so has Miss Jennie's school-house.

Mirador, however – the country mansion that Chillie acquired when he eventually made good – has not been pulled down, though it has passed out of the family and has not escaped the blight of over-zealous modernization. Its mellow pink brick has been sandblasted to a hectic red, and the drive has been asphalted right up to the front door. All the same it is still recognizably the place that Nancy loved above all others as a girl, and to which her thoughts increasingly returned towards the end of her life.

Chillie added two wings to the house which, though built in Colonial style, is of a rather later period, the 1820s. Even with his additions it is not, by English standards, a big house, seeming more manorial than stately. With its outhouses and dependent cottages it could, however, accommodate his family, servants and guests, as well as his horses and other livestock. It is part of a scattered rural community called Greenwood, the loveliest feature of which is the backdrop provided by the Blue Ridge Mountains.

Greenwood station was where the Langhornes used to get off when they

Greenwood, station for Mirador

The modern world comes to Mirador: Colonel Langhorne (right) looks at an early motor car, with the house behind

travelled, as they always did, by train from Richmond to Mirador, and Alice Winn has given us a detailed account of the journey which became such a familiar experience for Nancy:

At first the train travelled through the flat wooded country that lies to the west of Richmond until we reached Gordonsville, which was renowned for its fried chicken and lemon pies. After leaving Gordonsville the scenery improves and is undulating as far as Charlottesville. The train stopped at the lower station and then, with its engine bells clanging, slowly and sedately proceeded to the University station. After leaving Charlottesville the Blue Ridge came into sight and we reached our Promised Land. 'Wash' [the Pullman porter] called out the familiar names of the stations . . . Woods Crossing . . . Ivy Depot . . . Mechum's River . . . Crozet – now the train really started to climb. After 'Wash' called out the Greenwood Depot, he brushed us down from head to foot with a stiff

[21]

whiskbroom, and we went from the stuffy car into the bracing mountain air, descending the steep Pullman steps onto the footstool. The small station looked very friendly as the stationmaster came to welcome us. Making our way to the Mirador station wagon drawn by two horses, we climbed into its darkness and sat on benchlike seats, sniffing in the delicious smell of its patent leather curtains.

After Greenwood the train would go into a tunnel, the earliest made in the United States. Approaching the tunnel, it would give a high, wailing whistle, which was one of the sounds that Mirador-lovers best remembered. Then it would pass through the Rockfish Gap and down into the Shenandoah Valley.

At Mirador the Langhornes led the life of country gentry, Virginia-style. They hunted and competed in equestrian events. They entertained their neighbours and were, in return, entertained. In Virginia, as in South Carolina, much importance was attached to gracious living and the social superiority that it denoted. North Carolinans used to say that their state was a valley of modesty between two mountains of conceit, and perhaps they still have reason to say it.

To Nancy her early years at Mirador seemed, in retrospect, the happiest of her life. It was there that she grew from a girl to a young woman. Her eldest sister, Lizzie, was married and living in Richmond, and even Irene was of marriageable age when Mirador was acquired. But Nancy, at thirteen, was just the right age to enjoy the family's new home to the full. She loved riding and was soon a brave and highly competitive horsewoman, jumping big fences in the hunting field or show ring. She loved parties, and in due course began to appreciate the admiration of young men, though she was never too keen on physical contact with them. She loved her parents' black servants whom she regarded, in the traditional Southern way, as domestic pets, but whose droll or sentimental talk entranced her. She loved the games that she played with her brothers and sisters – one of which, the truth game (in which everybody said exactly what he or she thought of other people), was to become a lifelong addiction with her, and very much more than a game.

But there was also, from the first, a serious side to her nature; a yearning for spirituality and a desire to minister to those less fortunate than herself. The Langhornes were devout members of the Episcopalian Church, but Nancy was no ordinary church-goer. At one stage she dreamt of becoming a missionary, and she did become closely attached to a local clergyman, Archdeacon Frederick Neve, accompanying him on pastoral visits to the poor hill-farmers of the Blue Ridge. Through Neve she also got involved in working for a home for cripples and old people called 'The Sheltering Arms'.

In the younger generation of Langhornes good looks and charm were common to both sexes, but force of character was largely confined to the girls.

[22]

ABOVE *Nancy in her early teens: 'a yearning for spirituality'*
BELOW *Archdeacon Frederick Neve, towards the end of his life*

Nancy's brothers did not succeed in making much of their lives, and indeed two of them, Keene and Harry, died young. As Nancy's son Michael has written: 'They were intimidated by their father, and they both developed an overpowering attachment to the bottle.' But the Langhorne sisters were not crushed or cowed, and Nancy in particular had all her father's toughness. Observing the tendency among male members of her family to drink more than was good for them, she early formed the view that temperance was one of the worthiest of causes. When she once heard somebody in England say that she came of a long line of teetotallers, she was quick to remark: 'No, from a long line of drinkers.'

Irene was the outstanding beauty of the family, whose fame spread beyond Richmond and Albemarle County (where Mirador was situated); beyond, even, the State of Virginia. She opened the ball at the Philadelphia Assembly, was a queen of one of the Mardi Gras courts in New Orleans and, in 1894, was the first Southern debutante since the Civil War to be asked to lead the grand march at the

[24]

ABOVE *Irene Langhorne, drawn by her husband, Dana Gibson*
OPPOSITE *Nancy aged nineteen (photograph from which cameo on page 27 was taken)*

Patriarchs' Ball in New York. Chillie was immensely proud of her, and his pride was enhanced by her triumphs in the North. Americans have a healthy respect for power, and anti-Yankee sentiment did not exclude great satisfaction that his favourite daughter was proving such a success in Yankee high society. In a sense, he could feel that Irene was conquering the South's conquerors. She had more than sixty proposals of marriage, and her suitors would often try to ingratiate themselves with her by giving presents to her younger sisters. At last she accepted a proposal – from the artist Charles Dana Gibson – and they were married at St Paul's Church in Richmond in 1895. Chillie's objections were almost certainly less to the fact that Dana was a Yankee than to the idea of losing Irene to any man. He may also have doubted the capacity of an artist to keep her in the style to which he felt she was entitled, but on that score he need not have worried. Dana brought her not only wealth but national, even international, celebrity as an ideal figure of womanhood.

Irene's marriage was an important event in Nancy's life, because with it the spotlight switched to *her* as the eldest unmarried Langhorne girl. Never one to be upstaged, she began to play the part of a Southern belle with emulous zest. But her social career was as different from Irene's as their characters were different. She hated the young ladies' finishing school in New York, to which Irene had been a credit, and when she was sent to it her mutinousness gained her an early release.

Unlike Irene, Nancy did not have a formal coming-out – because, she says, she was 'supposed to be delicate' – but staying with the Gibsons and meeting their friends she was soon very much in the social swim. By the time she was seventeen she had already had that number of proposals, and the seventeenth she accepted. It was from a handsome, rich Bostonian 'of an old and distinguished family' (in Nancy's words). His name was Robert Gould Shaw II.

She met him at a polo match, where she was impressed by his courageous horsemanship. For his part, he was immediately attracted to her, and she was 'flattered and pleased to have made this spectacular conquest'. They became engaged and a little more than a year later, in October 1897, they were married quietly at Mirador. By worldly standards it was a 'good marriage', but in every essential respect it could hardly have been worse. Nancy claims to have had serious doubts about it in advance, but to have yielded to persuasion from 'the entire family' – though she admits that Chillie had a moment of uneasiness, which made him ask Shaw's father if he knew of any reason why his son should not marry. In fact, there was madness on the mother's side, which was not revealed to the Langhornes; but Chillie *was* informed that young Shaw had a record of dissipation, including drunkenness, which might well be no more than a passing phenomenon.

Apparently the Shaws made no secret of their hope that marriage to Nancy

Cameos of Nancy and Robert Gould Shaw II in a local paper at the time of their wedding

would have a sobering effect upon their Bob, and it is possible that this argument may have satisfied Chillie. He was not a man who could, without hypocrisy, have taken too censorious a line about liberal drinking. On the other hand there is a tradition among some members of the Langhorne family that Nancy's parents were dead against the marriage, and that she went through with it in spite of their fervent entreaties.

Whatever the truth about their attitude, they did not have to wait long for evidence that the marriage was going badly. After two days of honeymoon at Hot Springs, Virginia, Nancy was back at Mirador. Though she was prevailed upon, then, to return to her husband, and though they lived together for a time in Massachusetts, it soon became obvious that they were fatally incompatible. So far as he was concerned, being married to Nancy had the effect of aggravating rather than curing his drink problem, and this in turn increased her feeling of alienation from him.

The causes of marital breakdown are generally hard to establish with precision, and biographers are well advised to approach the matter with caution. But there are good grounds for believing that Nancy was, throughout her life, distinctly squeamish about the carnal aspects of marriage, and of course her temperament utterly rejected the role of decorative, submissive wife which Bob Shaw may have expected of her. It is said, too, that she teased him and laughed at him in the way that came so naturally to her, and that he found this insufferable.

At any rate, a deed of separation was signed in 1901, and Nancy was urged to divorce Bob on grounds sanctioned by American law if not by Holy Writ. But her

religious principles inhibited her and it was not until Bob's parents told her that he had secretly married another woman, and was in danger of being prosecuted for bigamy, that she agreed to divorce him, since she was then able to do so on the Biblical ground of adultery. The divorce was concluded in February 1903. It is only fair to add that Bob seems to have been reasonably happy and settled in his subsequent life.

There was one child of Nancy's first marriage – Robert Gould Shaw III, always known as Bobbie. He was born in 1898, and of all her children he was to remain the closest to her. So intimate was their relationship that her eldest Astor son, Bill, could remark that the umbilical cord uniting them was, in a sense, never cut. But there was much fever and pain, as well as mutual comfort, in their love for each other.

Nancy's divorce from Bob Shaw conveniently symbolizes the end of her early life in America. Already her compass-needle was turning towards England – and the fulfilment of her destiny.

Robert Gould Shaw III, 'Bobbie', at the time when he and his mother invaded England

2

England–
and Waldorf Astor

&⟨⟩

IN the late winter of 1903, immediately after her divorce, Nancy travelled to Europe with her mother and a friend, Alice Babcock (later Winthrop). They went first to France, and then to England where – in Nancy's own words – she had 'this strange feeling of having come home, rather than having gone abroad'.

But was the feeling so strange? She had, after all, received from Miss Jennie the most intensive indoctrination in all things English. Her school syllabus had been orientated far more towards England than towards her own country. For that reason alone it was hardly surprising that she loved her 'first glimpse of England and English ways'.

At Mirador, too, there had been influences making for Anglophilia. Nearby, at Ivy, there was a community of English immigrants to which Nancy's friend and mentor, Archdeacon Neve, belonged. The habits of this community included having English teas and playing cricket. There were also two young Englishmen in the district, Ned and Algy Craven, who had arrived there after the Langhornes, and who were more or less contemporaries of Nancy and her sister Phyllis. Their father had been master of the Pytchley, so they shared the Langhornes' love of horses and became almost members of the family. Later another Englishman (or rather Ulsterman), Angus McDonnell, came to work under Chillie on railroads and spent a lot of time at Mirador. He fell desperately in love with Nancy, but she would never have considered marrying him even if she had loved him, because he was only a younger son (of Lord Antrim) and had no money. All the same, she was fond of him and valued his friendship. But Nancy did not have to rely solely upon expatriates for contacts in England. Irene and Dana Gibson, after their marriage,

Nancy, conqueror of the hunting shires

[31]

had for a time lived in London, where they had taken a flat in the Albany and made many friends. Through them, Nancy had useful introductions on her first visit to what was to become her adopted country.

It should be remembered that England was still the cultural metropolis of the English-speaking world, and that her power, though increasingly threatened – not least by commercial competition from the United States – was still pre-eminent. The British social set-up had lost very little of its prestige, and the linguistic norm for all English-speaking people was still the King's rather than (as now) the President's English. East Coast Americans of 'good family' were particularly attracted to England, and to the extent that their values were rather snobbish they naturally felt a bit provincial by comparison with the English aristocracy. Yet the traditions of their own country also tended to make them somewhat resent the people and institutions that they admired, and to feel a certain moral superiority which compensated for their sense of social inferiority. In these respects, Nancy was the embodiment of a human condition that inspired much of the work of Henry James.

Seeing England for the first time was no disappointment to her. On the contrary, her interest in the country was further stimulated. Back in Virginia after a trip which did much to restore her morale, she suffered, in the late summer of 1903, her first painful bereavement, when her mother died suddenly at the relatively early age of fifty-five. Nancy was prostrated by the blow. She felt a sorrow such as she 'had never known or imagined', and was 'ill for months, in a wretched, nameless fashion'. But her basic stamina was more than equal to the emergency.

For a time she kept house for her father at Mirador, and did her best to fill the gap left by her mother's death. But the arrangement could never have lasted, because father and daughter were too much alike. Chillie was wise enough to see that Nancy had to be out in the world, making her own way. So he proposed, in 1904, that she should go to England for the hunting season, promising to join her there himself for Christmas.

She travelled, this time, with her favourite sister, Phyllis, next to her in age and an even better rider than she. Apart from Bobbie – who also accompanied her, with his nurse – Phyllis was probably the person she loved best and was certainly, for many years, her most intimate confidante. Unlike Nancy, Phyllis resembled their mother rather than Chillie. She lacked Nancy's confident, assertive, rather bullying character, but instead was sweet-natured with a touch of melancholy. Another difference was that she was very musical, whereas Nancy was tone-deaf.

But their temperaments were complementary, and besides they had much in common. In addition to all their shared experiences of childhood, Phyllis was now married, as Nancy had been, to a rich Northern socialite, with whom she was not

Ready to move off

happy and from whom she would later be divorced. Later still, she would marry an Englishman and settle, like Nancy, in England. In 1904, however, she was Mrs Reginald Brooks, with two sons, whom she took with her to England, as Nancy took Bobbie.

At first they stayed in London, at Fleming's Hotel in Half Moon Street. Then they moved to the best hunting country, taking a house outside Market Harborough, from which Nancy 'hunted hirelings of all shapes and sizes'. Whether in London or in the country she was an object of fascination. Her peculiar blend of outrageous talk and strictly moral behaviour acted as a puzzling but exciting challenge. The Edwardian *beau monde* soon accepted her on her own terms, as a young woman who was unnervingly fast in conversational attack and repartee, but not at all fast in the pejorative sense.

She began to make English friends, in some cases after a preliminary encounter which might not have led to friendship. When, for instance, General

[33]

Tom Holland offered to help her to remount after a fall, she shouted at him: 'Do you think I would be such an ass as to come out hunting if I couldn't mount from the ground?' But Holland did not hold it against her and they became great friends. When Mrs Gordon Cunard said to her: 'I suppose you've come over here to get one of our husbands', Nancy replied: 'If you knew the trouble I've had gettin' rid of mine, you'd know I don't want yours'. Mrs Cunard was captivated. Similarly, at a dance given by the Speaker of the House of Commons, Nancy left her partner in the middle of the floor, pirouetted up to someone, as yet a stranger to her, who was standing in a doorway, and abruptly asked: 'Do you love your husband?' The stranger was Anne Poynder (later Anne Islington) with whom she established a lasting rapport.

During her second visit to England she also fell in love. As in America, she had

The rejected suitor – John, Lord Revelstoke

proposals that she could refuse without a pang, including one from a Scottish peer who was so distressed at being rejected that he sought consolation in a long bout of big-game hunting. But Lord Revelstoke was another matter. His love for her, and hers for him, made her for a time – on her own admission – 'deliriously happy'. John Revelstoke did not suffer from the defect of being poor. He was head of the merchant banking house of Baring which, through his efforts, had recovered its prosperity and high standing after the crisis that had nearly destroyed it in 1890. He was, though prematurely bald, a man of consummate elegance, and his way of life was enhanced by having, as his cook, the now legendary Rosa Lewis.

If his devotion to Nancy, and the lustre of his position, had been combined with the intellectual sparkle and humorous eccentricity of his brother, Maurice Baring, it is likely that Nancy would have become Lady Revelstoke – and so, perhaps, known to history only as a name cropping up here and there in memoirs of the period. But unfortunately for him he was the sort of man whose words could not do justice to his feelings. The fact that he played the piano very well was wasted on Nancy.

Above all his position in the world, though advantageous in so many ways, was in one crucial respect against him. Nancy was not cut out to be the wife of a City magnate. When he warned her, very fairly, of the tedious social routine that she would have to face, he only succeeded in giving the impression that he doubted her ability to entertain royalty and other top people. This enabled her to write him off as 'an appalling snob', though if he had really been as snobbish as all that he would never, surely, have even considered an American divorcée as suitable to be his wife, let alone have courted her as ardently as he did. Nancy also managed to convince herself that, while protesting his love for her, he was secretly carrying on with another woman. 'I had taken it for granted that he was an unattached bachelor, but he wasn't. He had been having an affair that had gone on for years, with a married woman years older than I was.' The woman in question was Lady Desborough, and Revelstoke was certainly, like his brother Maurice, one of her numerous admiring men friends. But Nancy was probably wrong to suspect him of being her lover; his pleas of innocence ring true. Without knowing it, she may have been eager to find a good moral reason for not marrying him, when her actual reasons were more complex.

It may or may not have influenced her that Chillie, when he came over to England for Christmas, took an instant dislike to Revelstoke. Granted Nancy's wilful nature, one might suppose that her father could have done little more than reinforce doubts that she was already feeling herself. But if it was true that she married her first husband against his advice, she may have been rather more willing to be guided by him in the choice of a second. (One possible source of prejudice should be mentioned, though there is no evidence that it had anything to do with Nancy's decision. The Barings were Jewish, the Langhornes rather anti-Semitic.) In any case, when she returned to America in the summer of 1905, she wrote discouragingly, even brutally, to Revelstoke. But she did not decide against him finally until, in March of the following year, she decided in favour of another man. Revelstoke then accepted his fate with stoicism, and did not cease to be her friend. The genuineness of his love for her seems proved by the fact that he never married.

In a light-hearted way Nancy had discussed the problem of her re-marriage with English friends, and one of them, H.H. Asquith, wrote to her about it at Mirador, expressing his amused perplexity in verse:

> You must not reproach me, my dear Mrs Shaw;
> It's not like a Redskin selecting a squaw;
> For there's no tougher problem, in logic or law
> Than to find a fit mate for the lady called Shaw.

He had not, he said, abandoned the quest, but was becoming less hopeful of finding the right person, because in every candidate some vital quality seemed to be missing. 'Can it be that I am over-fastidious? Or even a little jealous? Impossible!' About a month after this characteristic letter was written Asquith was Chancellor of the Exchequer and Nancy had met her 'fit mate'. In December 1905 she returned to England for another hunting season. Her father accompanied her, and a fellow-passenger on the crossing was young Waldorf Astor, heir to one of the greatest fortunes in the world.

The Astors are of German origin, the founder of the dynasty, John Jacob Astor I, having been born the son of a village butcher at Walldorf, in Baden. It was later suggested that the family came originally from Spain, where the name was Astorga, and there has also been speculation that the Astorgas may have been Sephardic Jews. But there is no evidence to support these theories. The only certainty is that in the eighteenth century the Astors were German Lutherans living in decent obscurity. John Jacob I, however, emigrated first to England, and then to America at about the time of the Colonies' revolt. As a citizen of the infant Republic he built up a vast empire in a variety of trading enterprises and in real estate. The basis of his success was the fur trade, in which he was a pioneer, establishing the American and Pacific Fur Companies. He bought animal pelts dirt cheap from the Indians, often paying them in alcohol and thus contributing to the degeneration of an anyway doomed race. (Nancy used to talk of 'the skunk-skinnin' Astors' – but without them her own career in politics and philanthropy would never have occurred.) The fur trade led John Jacob I into ventures further afield, in Hawaii and then in China. But the permanence of Astor

[36]

The successful suitor – Waldorf Astor

Al fresco lunch under the pergola at Cliveden, about 1907

wealth was due to his foresight in investing so much of the profit from his commercial activities in land on Manhattan, so that his family became the chief beneficiary of the rapid growth of New York City. His descendants had only to sit tight and the money would continue, inexorably, to roll in.

Waldorf Astor was a great-great-grandson of the founding father. His own father, William Waldorf, had broken away from the family tradition of single-minded, Philistine money-grubbing. He had also broken away from the United States and returned to the Old World. By temperament a passionate, if rather lugubrious, romantic, he had forsaken the New York counting-house (though not its proceeds) to cultivate the tastes of a Renaissance prince and to found a branch of the Astor dynasty in England. As American envoy plenipotentiary in Italy he acquired many works of art and wrote a novel about the Borgias. But in 1890, having despaired of making a career for himself in American politics, he decided to move to England and become a British subject. He brought with him his handsome but shy and retiring wife – born Mary Dahlgreen Paul, of Philadelphia – and their four children, Waldorf, John Jacob V, Pauline and Gwendolyn (who died in childhood). One reason that he gave for leaving America was that he was afraid his children would be kidnapped, but his main reason was summed up in the

notorious statement, publicly reported at the time: 'America is not a fit place for a gentleman to live.'

In England he set about equipping himself and his family with the appurtenances of aristocracy. He bought two historic country places – Cliveden in Buckinghamshire and Hever Castle in Kent – on which he spent millions of dollars and which he filled with the treasures that he had collected. He also acquired a London house in Carlton House Terrace, and built an office in Tudor style on Victoria Embankment, in which, for security, all the doors had handles only on the outside and could be locked simultaneously by a central controlling mechanism. Feeling that newspaper ownership would help him to get on in English life, he acquired the *Pall Mall Gazette* and later – several years after Nancy and Waldorf married – the *Observer*. He did some entertaining, because he could see that it was the thing to do, and his wealth ensured that the smart English world would not entirely spurn his hospitality. But his parties were not festive occasions. At one of them he stopped the orchestra playing at 11 p.m., when many of the guests had only just arrived, and announced that the party was over because he wanted to go to bed.

His hopes of fulfilling his aristocratic dream were concentrated upon his children, whose lives he directed in solitude after their mother's death in 1894. He was an aloof, rather awe-inspiring parent, but he did his best for them according

Edwardians on the terrace at Cliveden

to his lights. His sons, in particular, were given every opportunity that he could think of to develop as English gentlemen, taking their place in the social order that he so admired.

It has been necessary to give this brief account of William Waldorf Astor, his background and aspirations, because without it the character of young Waldorf would be hard to understand. Like his brother John, he emerged a model (and therefore unnatural) English gentleman, but more truly a good American, and in a sense no less truly a good German. His English upper-class education disguised, but could not remove, characteristics that came to him from his heredity and home environment.

At Eton he was Captain of the Boats and Treasurer of Pop (the self-perpetuating social oligarchy which used to have, if it does not still have, more prestige in the eyes of Etonians than athletic or, certainly, academic success). He also edited the school magazine and won a prize for French – a language which he spoke well, thanks not to Eton but to private tuition, At New College, Oxford, he only got a fourth-class degree (in Modern History), but distinguished himself as a sportsman, representing the university at polo and fencing, and becoming Master of the Drag. He also belonged to the Bullingdon Club, another social élite.

On the face of it, he was a typical representative of the Edwardian *jeunesse dorée*. But on closer inspection he was not typical at all. He lacked altogether the easygoing casualness and the sometimes (though not very often) deceptive amateurishness of the English upper class. At heart he was an excessively serious young man, with a puritan conscience and a mania for method. Even his recreations were made to seem more like work than play. He was a born planner.

His son Michael has written of the Astors: 'A heavy Germanic quality, inherited from the male line, coupled with a conscientious form of Lutheran orthodoxy, seemed to have deprived them of a sense of fun.' This was true up to a point of Waldorf – but only up to a point. Though not really humorous himself, he was capable of enjoying the effects of humour, rather as an uneducated man can appreciate the effects of learning.

He was also remarkably kind, and he had a smile that no one who knew it can ever forget. People who worked for him or with him invariably liked and respected him. He might almost have been atoning for the systematic nastiness of his ancestor who created the family fortune, by being systematically nice.

Addicted though he was to planning, his life was not going according to plan at the time he met Nancy. Ill-health had struck him and turned him into a semi-invalid. He had been found to have a weak heart, and he was also suspected of tuberculosis. This meant that he had to give up all the strenuous sports in which he was so proficient, and for the time being he was just a very rich young man with noble ideals and nothing in particular to do. As such, he was very much better suited to Nancy than John Revelstoke would have been. Revelstoke had great wealth (though not as great as Waldorf's), but he was also committed to an occupation and a way of life which would have denied Nancy the freedom that her nature required. Waldorf, despite his education, was by no means a settled member of the British establishment. Like Nancy, he had an American background. He was also good-looking and as young as she was. (It is always said that they were exactly the same age, both having been born on 19 May 1879. But Nancy's Danville birth certificate shows that she was, in fact, two days older.)

Nancy does not describe how exactly they met on the boat, but she does say that Waldorf intended to marry her even before he met her, and that when she delayed seeing him because she was feeling a bit sea-sick he employed his time working on Chillie. 'A clever man can always find more ways than one of getting what he wants. Waldorf knew all the ways. [He had] immense courtesy and very great personal charm. He soon had Father eating out of his hand.' By contrast

Revelstoke may, unconsciously, have given Chillie the impression that he was slightly high-hatting a rough American.

When she reached England for her third visit Nancy continued to see Waldorf, but was in no hurry to bring matters to a head. Her immediate interest was the hunting season, during which for part of the time she hunted with the Beaufort rather than with the Fernie, as previously.

A document in the Astor archive at Reading University gives us some idea of the paraphernalia involved in serious hunting during the Edwardian period. One of Nancy's grand friends in the East Midlands, Sir Humphrey de Trafford, sent her a list of items that he was despatching, with her horses and a groom (paid twenty-seven shillings a week), to Badminton. Here is the list, which reads more like the equipment for a unit of cavalry than for one young woman:

1 long cheap newly-mounted bridle with port and gag	2 chamois
4 head collars	2 body brushes
2 prs. knee caps	2 curry combs
2 tail guards	2 prime Turkey sponges
2 set white wool bandages	2 mane combs
1 sandwich case for sandwich box	12 rubbers
1 leather case for flask	oil
3 nummers	2 gall. sand bag
1 saddle pad	burnisher
2 rollers	2 super quality fawn sheets bound cloth
2 rugs	2 super blankets
2 kerseys	2 super woollen rollers
3 stirrup leathers and irons	2 bt. girths & straps
3 double rein bridles	2 sets linen bandages
1 snaffle	2 sets woollen bandages
1 child's snaffle	2 prs. best leather knee caps
2 ring martingales	2 best leather tail cases
2 saddle boxes	4 full-size super fawn hods bound scarlet cloth
1 child's saddle complete	2 best hand knitted white wool withers pads
2 side saddles, no girths	
2 best dandies	2 prs. best extra thick white swabs
2 water brushes	2 prs. super Fitz girths with buff chapes

One can only hope that Nancy thoroughly enjoyed the hunting season of 1905–6, because it was to be her last. After she married Waldorf he would never allow her to hunt. It was a sport that he could not share with her, because it was one of those that he had been forced to give up. No doubt he feared, above all, for her safety, but even with him there may have been more selfish, subsidiary motives, including a little jealousy of her hunting friends.

Her thoughts on the subject of marriage crystallized as the hunting season was drawing to an end. Early in March 1906 she decided to marry Waldorf, and it was certainly a wise decision. Though she was not swept off her feet by him – as Alice Winn says, she was less in love with him than he with her – she loved him well enough to make a go of the partnership. Without the Astor millions he would not have had a chance, and she always frankly admitted that his vast wealth was one of her reasons for marrying him. But she would never have married him for that alone. She could see that their qualities were in many ways complementary – that he was almost ideally suited to act as the 'straight man' to her inspired comedy, while on the serious side his patient, methodical mind could provide indispensable backing for her missionary flair. She also felt, and this was most important to her, that he would be a good stepfather to Bobbie.

Nancy after her marriage to Waldorf, wearing a tiara with the Sanci diamond

All the same she hesitated. Clearly she could not afford to make a second mistake, and after her experience with Shaw she was naturally rather chary of marriage. But at last she gave her consent, and the precipitating cause may have been an appeal from Crown Princess (as she then was) Marie of Rumania. Waldorf's father was a friend of the King and Queen of Rumania, with whom he and his children stayed. The Crown Princess, unhappily married, was probably in love with Waldorf, and he was certainly very fond of her. But when she realized, from correspondence, that he was infatuated with Nancy, she had the generosity to write to Nancy and plead with her to marry him. While resenting the intrusion, Nancy was also alerted to what she may have felt to be a potential challenge. At all events she promptly made up her mind in favour of Waldorf.

There remained considerable anxiety as to how his father would react. Nancy was not the virginal British aristocrat that he must have been hoping for as a

Waldorf (third from right) giving Rumanian guests tea at Cliveden, 5 August 1902
Princess Marie is wearing the white hat (third from left)

daughter-in-law, but a Virginian divorcée with a six-year-old child. With some misgivings the couple visited him at Sorrento, where he happened to be staying, only to find that their fears were groundless. William Waldorf Astor took an immediate liking to Nancy and gave the marriage his blessing. This was not only an act of spiritual grace: in due course it took very tangible forms. Mr Astor handed over Cliveden to his son as a wedding present, together with a huge financial settlement to enable him to keep it up. His present to Nancy was the famous Sanci diamond, which had belonged to James I and Charles I, and which later had been worn by Louis XIV at his coronation.

Nancy was determined to be married in church, and she obtained the necessary authorization from the Bishop of London. But her second wedding, like her first, was very quiet. She and Waldorf were married at All Souls Church, Langham Place, on 3 May 1906. Neither of their parents was able to attend (each having gout, Chillie back in America) and both the date and venue were kept a secret from the Press.

The couple went to Cortina in Switzerland for their honeymoon, and this time Nancy did not run away.

3

Fashionable Saint

❧

IN becoming Mrs Waldorf Astor, Nancy secured a position which her own talents and personality were able to enhance beyond measure. She also acquired a husband whose devotion to her was complete.

It must not be thought that Waldorf was the male equivalent of a squaw. In his quiet way he was a strong and stubborn, even a dominant, character. In marrying Nancy he, too, got what he wanted, and it was due to Fate rather than to any design on his part that she later became a world celebrity to whom he appeared to be no more than a loving appendage. Aware of his own limitations, he felt the need for her brilliance and uninhibited vitality. Without her, his life would have been dull in every sense, and he knew it. Yet he did not underrate his own ability nor was he without ambition. On the contrary, he intended to make as much of his life as his health would permit, and it seemed to him that with Nancy at his side he could achieve much that would otherwise be beyond him.

Despite his physical weakness he decided, with her support, to go into politics. Though he might well have become a Liberal of the new, social-reforming type, he chose instead to be a left-wing Conservative. But he refused the offer of a safe seat and in 1908 was adopted as a candidate in Plymouth, which was not at all a promising area. In the general election of January 1910 he was defeated, but in the second election of that year, in December, he was elected. Thus began a long political association between the Astors and Plymouth, from which the city benefited incalculably.

As an MP's wife Nancy took a very active interest in Plymouth, as we shall see. But – to return to the time of her marriage – her first task was to establish herself as the mistress of Cliveden, and this she did in the most unmistakable fashion. In her own words, the keynote when she went there was 'splendid gloom', but she improved the place at once by putting in 'books and chintz curtains and covers, and flowers'.

[47]

Nancy in 1909

Waldorf the candidate, Nancy the candidate's wife, Plymouth 1910

Mother had a coloured maid at Mirador, who used to go out into the garden and pick flowers and put them all mixed up in a big bowl. I told the gardener at Cliveden to send me someone to do the flowers every day. He sent me a man who was very good at it. I showed him French prints and we began to do the flowers like that. Soon a lot of people were copying.

Cliveden is marvellously situated, with a commanding view of the Thames near Maidenhead and of an expanse of outer suburbia which, by some miracle, looks like country. The property has often changed hands since George Villiers, 2nd Duke of Buckingham, built the first house on the site in Restoration times. The house acquired by Waldorf's father from the Duke of Westminster was the third, and the main part of it was designed by Sir Charles Barry in the mid-nineteenth century. Barry of course also designed, in a very different style, another building with which Nancy was to be closely associated: the House of Commons.

In fairness to William Waldorf Astor, it should be said that he did much for Cliveden. Inside, he enlarged the entrance hall to its present dimensions, and obtained for the wall facing the front door tapestries made for the house at an earlier period, but dispersed at the end of the eighteenth century. He also created a Louis xv dining room with panelling, decoration and furniture brought or copied from the Château d'Asnières, not far from Paris.

His most striking achievements, however, were outside the house, where the fruits of his 'Italian period' are much in evidence. The long balustrade below the house on the side overlooking the river, together with seats, statues and small fountains, was brought from the Villa Borghese in Rome – transported thence

OPPOSITE ABOVE *The Borghese balustrade, brought to Cliveden by William Waldorf Astor*
BELOW *The hall at Cliveden, with Nancy's portrait by Sargent to the left of the fireplace*

by sea and up the Thames to Cliveden. A magnificent Italianate fountain at the end of the straight drive approaching the house was placed there by William Waldorf, and other classical objects acquired by him adorn the grounds.

Nancy's contribution to Cliveden was less monumental, but more life-giving. The Langhornes were gifted with visual taste which came out most strongly in the eldest sister, Lizzie, but which was also quite marked in Nancy herself. She had an eye for beautiful things and, having the means to buy more or less anything she wanted, was a fairly active buyer, particularly of china, for the rest of her life. But above all she knew how to brighten a house, and whereas Waldorf's father had turned Cliveden into a sort of mausoleum, she turned it into an omnium–gatherum.

Her style of entertaining there did not come fully into its own until after the Great War, but even in the early years of her marriage she asserted her own distinctive notions of hospitality, which derived from her home background rather than from British aristocratic models. She liked to mix her guests as she mixed flowers. Though not free from snobbishness – whatever she might think – about ancient and, more especially, royal families, and though always liable to be interested in celebrities for celebrity's sake, she did not confine her attention to the well-born, rich and famous, but asked many people to stay who would never otherwise have found themselves in such company.

Cliveden was by no means the only place where the Astors lived and entertained. A few years after they were married Waldorf bought 4 St James's Square, which remained their London house until after the Second World War. It was large enough to meet all their requirements, for work as well as for play, and when they moved into it Nancy's only complaint (in a letter to a friend) was that, being in a corner of the square, it created difficulties for the horses when people were arriving in carriages for a party.

Even before his election to Parliament Waldorf acquired a fine house in Plymouth, 3 Elliot Terrace, on the Hoe. Here the Astors received local friends and worthies, and here they put up visiting VIPs, throughout their long association with the city.

In 1911 Nancy felt the need for 'a cottage by the sea', so with the help of an architect she planned Rest Harrow at Sandwich Bay. In fact it turned out to be a house with fifteen bedrooms, but at least it was a good deal smaller than Cliveden. The atmosphere was intimate, and Nancy loved the place, as did other members of the family. Soon one of the most important events in her life was to occur there.

Part of every summer Waldorf liked to spend in the Scottish Highlands, where he stalked and fished with the relentless application that he brought to anything that he did. Eventually he acquired an estate on the island of Jura, but during the years before 1914 he took a succession of lodges. Nancy at first tried to convince

[51]

The dining-room at Cliveden, with a bust of Madame de Pompadour

herself that the Highlands were good for her, but later she came to regard staying there as a penance.

As well as moving from place to place in Britain, the Astors used to spend some of their time in foreign resorts, such as St Moritz or Biarritz. Direct contact with the French did nothing, however, to change her view of Latin people generally, whom she always found 'difficult to understand', because they had a 'set of moral values' permitting them 'to be proud about, and boast of, things no other man would be anything but heartily ashamed of'.

Nancy, Bobbie and (left) a French friend of Waldorf, picnicking in the Highlands

Nancy fishing at Loch Luichart

Between her marriage and the outbreak of the Great War Nancy gave birth to three Astor children – William Waldorf (Bill) in 1907, Phyllis (Wissie) in 1909 and David in 1912. Child-bearing seems to have aggravated the tendency to ill-health for which she had always been noted, and, despite the many social activities and triumphs of her early married life, for most of that time she was treated, and advised to treat herself, more or less as an invalid.

Hitherto there has been little to illuminate her state of mind during a period that was certainly formative in her career, but now it is possible to show exactly what the young Mrs Astor was privately thinking and feeling. From the letters – never before available to a biographer – written by her with great frequency and regularity to her beloved sister Phyllis, a most vivid picture of Nancy emerges. They reveal the inwardness of her character as nothing else has done. Phyllis, in America, is given all the London gossip, and it is clear that part of Nancy exults in the bright, smart world in which she has become a leading figure. But it is equally clear that another part of her despises it. 'You can't think what a rush London is in July. There are balls every second & something to do every minute. Nearly everyone rides in the Row at 10 o'c. They are strong but then they all go off to the country from now on till next season.'

When Waldorf says he is determined on the simple life for his children, she agrees with him and thinks it necessary, but:

. . . first one must get rid of servants. I sh. like to build a series of huts & one common dining room & kitchen. Still I won't bore you with my theories. Luxuries leave me so cold. I like them but I never really feel in the least dependent on them . . . and I know when socialism does come I shall be a *v* good house wife!

In fact, she continued to be ministered to by droves of servants, and the nearest she got to the simple life was Rest Harrow. Yet it *was* true that she could have done without luxuries, and that her personality would no more have been crushed by material adversity than her father's was.

Her disinclination to be a slave to luxury was genuine, but when it came to the point, less powerful than her resolve never again to be a slave to the poverty that she had witnessed and experienced in early childhood. Hence the contradiction in her, and the apparent hypocrisy. In theory she wanted to be independent of wealth, but in practice she regarded wealth as the only guarantee of independence. Thus she could admire somebody else who made an unworldly marriage. 'The girl Winston Churchill is [to] marry is *lovely* but *v* stupid. As poor as a rat – but nice. Everyone said he would only marry for ambition – this proves them wrong.' But she knew that she would never have made such a marriage herself. 'Think Phyl how rich Waldorf may be some day [he was rich enough already in all conscience] & think of the joy of knowing you are *absolutely* independent! It is comforting – I sh. have married an ogre for that!'

Waldorf was very far from being an ogre, and she would not, of course, have married him if he had been one. She acknowledged her luck, but without glossing over points of incompatibility or the difficulty, for her, of being *anybody's* wife. 'God has given me such a light & airy disposition &, oh my, what a husband! He's not absolutely perfect – no men are – but he's far better than any man I know. Only when he's tired he gets "crossish" which is so odd for him I can't make it out.'

In another letter: 'Waldorf's a man in 10,000 but he's got his stonewall [word missing] & I keep knocking into them & they bruise – still perhaps that's my fault & I sh. just be on the look out for cracks & bruises – but somehow I am not built on the Harem pattern. Any woman sh. be to make a perfect wife.' Again: 'One needs much prayer in matrimony – I admire Waldorf's will – but feel I sh. like to be able sometimes to resist it – *but* I won't.'

In a letter from Loch Luichart in Ross-shire she writes: 'Waldorf busy all day long which is a blessing but I can't get used to sharing my bed with anyone & some day I shall be firm about that.' No doubt Waldorf had to make some concessions to her will. But on most issues he got his way, and it is interesting to find that his anti-Popish bigotry exceeded hers. From Loch Luichart again: 'There's a heavy mist &

[55]

Nancy in 1913 with (left to right), Wissie, Bobbie, David and Bill

Waldorf won't go to the RC church where I feel the bright candles wd. cheer me. So we must go to the Kirk.'

During the pre-1914 years a most unusual Roman Catholic entered her life and became her closest friend. Philip Kerr, later Lord Lothian, was also very close to Waldorf, and Nancy thought him a good influence. 'I must say Phillip [*sic*] comes nearer making Waldorf talk than anyone I have ever known. That is a godsend.' And: '[Waldorf] is becoming very religious & much more spiritually inclined – I put this down to Phillip.'

If Kerr's Roman Catholicism had been securely based he would have been unlikely to appeal to Waldorf. But in fact it was very shaky, whereas his secular faith in the British Empire, which Waldorf shared, was by comparison robust. An intellectual and disciple of Lord Milner, to whose 'Kindergarten' in South Africa he had belonged, he was a strange, cranky and casuistical, but also humorous and delightful, man. Nancy was fascinated by him, and her letters to Phyllis are full of laudatory references to him. From St Moritz: 'I am becoming a better woman since seeing so much of Phillip Kerr. I fear he will eventually be a priest. He certainly has the true spirit of a Christian. Such sympathy, such understanding.' Again, from the same address: 'You will read a lot of Phillip Kerr in my letters. He says that this life doesn't count – that it is only the supernatural side that matters & things that you actually do here don't count, only your intentions. . . . He hates to think of Heaven as a sort of Reward.' Nancy is impressed by such spirituality, but adds, disarmingly, that she prefers to think of Heaven as 'a pageant in gold'.

Kerr did not confine himself to the higher regions of mind and spirit or she would have found him a bore. 'Everything he does he does well – at golf he is scratch.' In the same letter, from Biarritz, Nancy shows that she is trying to keep up with him: 'I am becoming quite good at golf. My putting is bad otherwise I drive & approach fairly well.' She never became anything like scratch, but played the game with much enjoyment, and rather surprising steadiness, until well into old age. It was, for her, one of the attractions of Sandwich.

People have asked, and are entitled to ask, if she and Philip Kerr were lovers, in the ordinary, non-Platonic sense. The overwhelming probability is that they were not. For one thing, Nancy's religious belief in marital fidelity was apparently helped by the relative absence of temptation. 'To be free of one's evil passions is well worth fighting for. God has been kind to you Phyllis & me, & I feel we don't have many struggles in that line.' But virtue may have received assistance from another, more disturbing, facet of Nancy's character. When, towards the end of her life, she was asked pointblank by her niece, Nancy Lancaster, if there had been anything physical between her and Philip, she replied that there had not been – because if there had, she would have lost her hold on him. Extreme possessiveness was, indeed, one of her strongest traits, and if in this case it helped to restrain an adulterous impulse, moralists have a tough problem to unravel. The only certainty is that a special relationship developed between her and Philip, from which Waldorf was not excluded, but in which, on the contrary, he featured to the extent of making it a sort of *ménage à trois* – though not in the usual sense of the term.

There can be no doubt that Nancy's religious hankerings were stimulated by Philip, as his were by her. In another letter from Biarritz she writes to her sister:

I am becoming *v devout*. I feel the need of prayer & Church. I feel unless I am careful I shall be going backwards instead of forward. God has been so good to us & I don't do half enough. I sh. try to make myself into a sort of fashionable saint! So look out . . . you may find yourself in the presence of a *v* good woman for a change.

Her Christianity was bound to be more active than contemplative. Kneeling was not a posture that came naturally to her, as she admits, in effect, when she says in an earlier letter: 'I am sure God means us to use Humility with discretion.' In that sense, if in no other, her discretion was impeccable.

But in the warmth of her response to other human beings, particularly to those in need, she was a true and natural Christian. For instance, she tells Phyllis: 'Tomorrow I entertain 26 girls from the East End – poor workers. I am greatly looking forward to it.' The most striking words are the last. Other grand ladies, though not many, might have given a treat to East End girls, but most of them would have done it as a tedious chore rather than as a labour of love.

From Plymouth she writes: 'Visited all this a.m. I only visit the poor &, oh Phyl, they are poor. I match them against our mountain poor.' She is remembering her missionary treks with Archdeacon Neve. On another occasion, in the train returning from Plymouth, she deplores having to leave early because Waldorf is ill. 'I hate giving up things in Plymouth. I had 4 more days' work. But when Waldorf is ill I am miserable.'

How many Tory (or Liberal) MPs' wives of the period were getting so deeply involved in their husbands' constituencies or reacting to the spectacle of poverty as she did?

I have no news – only a heavy heart at all the poverty I saw in Plymouth. Yesterday a tea to street waifs. One poor little consumptive cripple & his father gets 7/– a week & had 6 children! It makes one think – there must be something *v* wrong with civilization which allows such things.

She adds, however, that a lot of the trouble is due to idleness and drink, and that she is 'a stronger teetotaller than ever'.

Working with and for others took her out of herself, and must have been a

Nancy resting, during her period of ill-health before Christian Science changed her life

welcome change from the routine of rest that her doctor, Sir Bertrand Dawson, imposed. She was impatient of this, but not yet to the point of rebellion. 'Well darlingest Phyl, I must as ever rest. It's a bore this constant resting.' Again: 'Never relax. It's absolute misery. I am relaxed. I just ache & lie like a log. I might just as well be dead as alive. I take no interest in anything & am numb in body and mind.'

Early in 1914 she became really ill with an internal abscess. Dawson insisted that she be operated on and after the operation she went to Sandwich to recover. There she had an experience akin to that of St Paul on the road to Damascus.

I had a nurse to look after me, and I lay in the sunshine on the balcony that looks out over the sea. The world was so lovely and so peaceful, and I began to argue with myself as I lay there. This, I thought, is not what God wants. . . . It couldn't be that God made sickness. It turned people into useless self-centred people who became a burden to themselves and everyone else. I lay for hours there, puzzling it out with myself.

Then a wonderful thing happened. Whenever a soul is ready for enlightenment, and awaits it humbly, I believe that the answer is somewhere to hand; the teacher comes.

The teacher, in her case, was a Christian Science enthusiast, Maud Bull, whose visit was arranged by Phyllis – ironically, because Phyllis was never herself a Christian Scientist. Maud Bull converted Nancy there and then to Christian Science; or rather, she gave Nancy a systematic framework for what she already believed.

She told me . . . there were people in America who believed, as I did, that God never meant there to be sickness and suffering, and who could be cured by prayer. I was deeply impressed and in a way comforted, for it was a confirmation of something I had felt instinctively must be.

Those passages, in Nancy's unpublished memoir, say it all. In supposing that she was 'humbly' waiting for enlightenment, she was deceiving herself. In reality, she was waiting for the means to institutionalize, as it were, her own innate self-confidence. Christian Science merely confirmed her belief that God was responsible only for what was good in Creation and that evil things, including sickness, must be due to human weakness and error.

No doubt it was a further attraction of Christian Science that it came from 'people in America'. Nancy always felt herself to be a breath of American fresh air in the stuffy Old World, and the fact that Christian Science was an American re-interpretation of Christianity (though emanating, regrettably, from Boston, Mass., rather than from Virginia) was bound to be in its favour, so far as she was concerned. For Nancy, Christian Science was the answer, because it perfectly suited her own physical and mental nature. Despite her reputation for ill-health, she was, in fact, as strong as an ox. Her troubles must have been psychological rather than organic, and of course a vigorous mental attitude ('holding the right thought') can go far towards curing such troubles.

After her decisive encounter with Maud Bull she submitted, under protest, to a second operation, but thereafter said good-bye to doctors and medicines, and hardly knew another day's serious illness until the end of her life. She was able to practise what she preached, because in this respect, too, she was largely free from temptation (in the form of bodily weakness or disease).

Her conversion to Christian Science was good for her morale, providing a total release for energies which had been, at least partly, pinioned. But it in no way

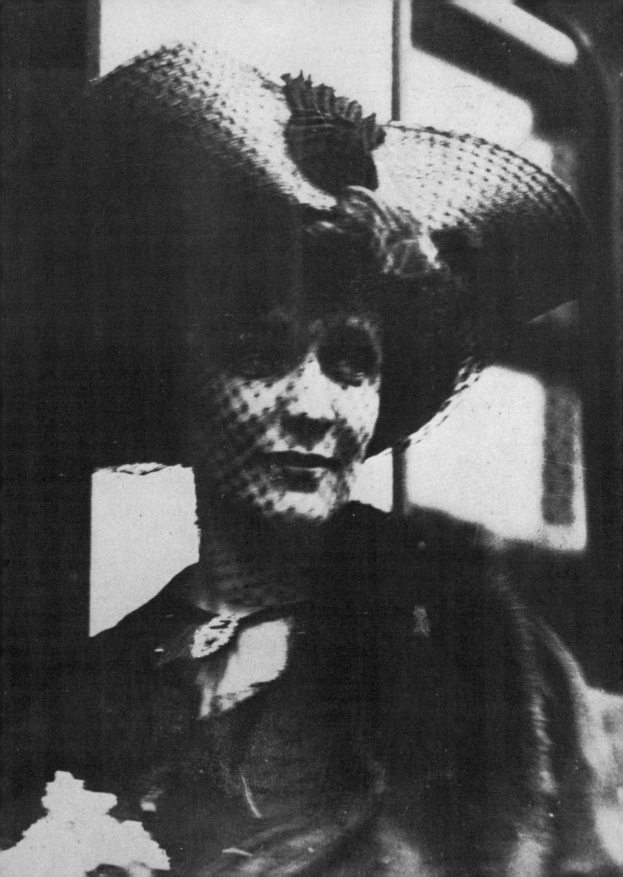

resolved the basic tension in her life, between the socialite and the social crusader.

It had, moreover, two very bad effects. One was that it reinforced, one could almost say sanctified, her natural tendency to be intolerant of people and ideas that she did not understand. When strong religious feeling is imprisoned in dogma, the result is bigotry. From 1914 onwards Nancy had all the intolerance that goes with religious fanaticism, though mercifully it was softened in her case by natural humanity and humour. The other bad effect of her conversion was that it deprived her of the opportunity for wide general reading that her periods of enforced leisure had given her. In her letters to Phyllis there are many allusions to books, which show a lively, if idiosyncratic, interest in literature. Her advice is: 'Read good novels – don't try essays or poetry – it's not exciting enough.'

The novels that she recommends include *Tom Jones*, Arnold Bennett's *Clayhanger*, and Anatole France's *Thaïs*. She also reports that she is reading *Pride and Prejudice* for the second time, with this rather ludicrous comment: 'It's *v* quaint & almost uncreditable [*sic*] to believe such stiff foolish people ever existed.' But it was, surely, creditable on her part that she was reading the book a second time in her early thirties. (Winston Churchill did not read it for the first time until 1943, when he was nearly seventy.) Among other books that she mentions are the life of Danton by her friend Hilaire Belloc and the *Life of Jesus* by Renan. It would be too much to describe her as bookish before 1914, but at least she spent a good deal of time reading books. After she became a Christian Scientist she allowed herself very little time for reading anything except the Bible and Mrs Eddy's *Science and Health*.

Within weeks of her own conversion she had converted Philip Kerr, who then intensified, over the years, her prejudice against Roman Catholicism, since he reacted against his old faith with all the violence of an apostate. But it took her ten years to convert Waldorf.

Nancy in July 1914, soon after her conversion to Christian Science

4

Easy Ride
to Westminster

&⸱⸱

THE spiritual crisis that changed Nancy's life was soon followed by an
international crisis that changed the world. In August 1914 what is still
called the Great War began, and by the time it was over even the
victorious nations had undergone profound changes – one of which, in England,
was to affect Nancy's future decisively.

Many of her friends were killed in the war, but not her very closest nor any
member of her family. Waldorf's weak heart disqualified him from combatant
service, and Bobbie never went to the front, though he became an officer in the
'Blues' (Royal Horse Guards). Philip Kerr decided that it was right for him to
keep out of the fighting. Christian Scientists were 'all at sixes and sevens about the
war' (he wrote to Nancy), but those with 'enough understanding of the truth'
would not fight, and he was one of them. Yet he did not condemn the war as such,
and later became private secretary to Lloyd George as war leader. His philosophy
was that pacifism, like patriotism, was not enough.

Nancy's response to the war was less convoluted, though on the face of it
rather odd for a Christian Scientist. Her principal war work was in the Canadian
Red Cross Hospital which was established at Cliveden. The house itself was
considered unsuitable for the purpose, but the big covered tennis court about a
mile away was converted into the hospital, while the adjacent Taplow Lodge was
used to accommodate the staff. At first the hospital could hold only about a
hundred patients, but in due course it was enlarged to hold more than six
hundred. Nancy says that, by the end of the war, twenty-four thousand had
passed through it. The figure may be a bit exaggerated, but it is no exaggeration to
describe her as the hospital's good angel.

She was not only a constant visitor to the wards, cheering the wounded with
her beauty, breeziness and humour. She also brought a variety of well-known

[63]

Nancy with Isaac Foot, her Liberal opponent in the 1919 by-election

Nancy with Colonel Newbourne, commandant of the hospital at Cliveden

personalities to talk to them or to entertain them, ranging from Rudyard Kipling to George Robey. One of these 'guest artists' was a Labour friend of hers, J.H. Thomas – trade union leader and, later, Labour Cabinet Minister – with whom she had a bantering exchange which shows both the quickness of her wit and the sort of fun she was able to provide for the patients.

Thomas, who often stayed at Cliveden, either in the house or in a cottage on the estate that the Astors lent him, suggested talking about what Labour would do with the Cliveden estate, if it were elected to power. Nancy immediately commented: 'That will be very interestin'. I have always wanted to know that. My own suggestion is that you turn it into a boardin'-house and make me the landlady; though in that case, Mr Thomas, you'll have to pay your board, a thing you've never done in the past.'

She got on very well with the hospital commandant, Colonel Newbourne, a Canadian with roots in Yorkshire. In her own words:

He was a wonderful surgeon and a very great gentleman. He was fearless and unconventional, and had a great sense of humour. He also had what's not always the professional surgeon's trademark – immense kindliness. He and I worked together. . . . (It was a love at first sight match!) We made the hospital not only the best in the kingdom, but also the happiest. I knew that every man in the place would get as good treatment as the Prince of Wales himself could have got. When there was a serious case, Colonel Newbourne would visit the man himself two or three times every night.

Such was Nancy's regard for the Colonel that, when he was exhausted at the end of a long day, she would give him mint juleps, made by herself, on the terrace at Cliveden. He was 'the only living man' for whom she would have done such a thing, because mint julep was a strong drink. It was one of her father's favourites, and she made it according to his formula – liquid sugar with a few mint leaves, crushed ice, bourbon whisky, more ice, then a few more sprigs of mint.

But she lectured the patients on temperance, and years later, speaking in New York, she described the type of lecture she gave and how one of the patients reacted:

I began with a picture of Canada, their mothers, their sweethearts at home, and what they wished and prayed for them. Then I would paint a picture of what having a 'grand time' meant – drink, women, etc., and then the awful consequences which so often followed a 'grand time' – sometimes prison, sometimes worse than prison, nearly always misery. They would listen because they knew I cared. . . . One boy came up to me as he was going on leave, after one of my horrible talks, gave me his money and said: 'Here, Mrs Astor, you've just ruined my holiday'.

Nancy recruited local ladies, each to be responsible for one ward, supplying it with books and flowers and taking the patients out for drives, or giving tea-parties

[65]

The war cemetery at Cliveden, with symbolic figure on left (the head was modelled on Nancy's)

for them when they were convalescing. But if a patient was not recovering and orthodox medicine seemed to be at the end of its resources, there was no one to compete with Nancy's form of shock treatment.

There were two sailors who had come [in] after the battle of Jutland. They were so badly wounded that they had turned their faces to the wall and given up. They were not expected to live.

'They don't want to,' the doctor told me. 'No one can do anything with them.'

I went along to see them. I asked them where they came from.

'Yorkshire,' said one of them.

I said 'No wonder you don't want to live, if you come from Yorkshire!'

One of the men raised himself on an elbow.

'Repeat that!' he said. Yorkshire, he pointed out, was the finest place in the world and if I said otherwise it meant I knew nothing about it. To hell with the battle of Jutland, he said. He was going back to Yorkshire – and he did!

From time to time Colonel Newbourne would come to me and say: 'Here is someone I can do nothing with. You take him on.' Then I would pray and keep my ammunition dry! I would take over. I remember a young Canadian who couldn't take it. He too had given up.

'I'm going to die,' he said.

I said 'Yes, Saunders, you're going to die. You're going to die because you have got no guts. If you were a Cockney or a Scot or a Yank, you'd live. But you're just a Canadian, so you'll lie down and die! I'll have them send you up a good supper for your last meal and I bet you this wrist watch you'll be dead this time tomorrow. You can keep it till then,' I said. 'I'll get it back when you're gone.'

He ate the supper I sent him, and he still has the watch. Later when he got back home he wrote me from the Middle West.

'They're making a lot of me here,' he said. 'They think I'm a hero. Gee, Mrs Astor, they don't know how much you had to kick me around to make me live!'

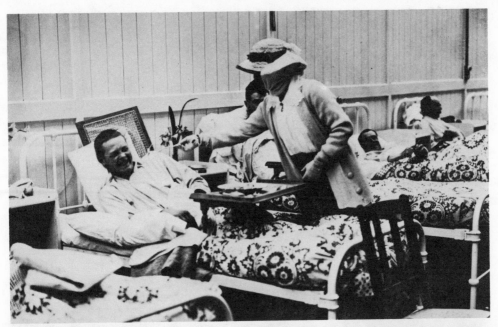

[67]

ABOVE *Nancy administering her form of shock treatment to the wounded*
BELOW *Nancy with a group of convalescent wounded, one doing the embroidery that she so strongly advocated*

Four 'graduates' of the Cliveden hospital; captions by Waldorf, though one by Nancy,
'Strawberry a wag and wit – took to drink after the war'

To some patients in a desperate state Nancy's technique could have been the *coup de grâce*, and history does not relate how many – if any – succumbed. Naturally enough, her own account tells only of the quasi-miraculous cures. One has to hope that Colonel Newbourne used discrimination in his choice of guinea-pigs for her.

Forty Canadians who died in the hospital, and two nursing sisters, are buried in a war cemetery in the garden at Cliveden. It is dominated by the statue of a female figure with outstretched arms, which is supposed to represent Canada. But in fact the head is Nancy's. The sculptor, Bertram MacKennal, had recently done a head of her, and he used it as the model for his symbolical figure.

At Plymouth, too, Nancy visited war hospitals, and it was there that she 'started the men embroidering and knitting' – a form of occupational therapy which, she claims, had not been thought of before. In a naval hospital at Plymouth a blinded seaman recognized her voice from having heard it, about ten years previously, on a transatlantic liner, when Nancy got into conversation one night with members of the crew. She always used to say it was that conversation that had first revealed to her her capacity to establish rapport with ordinary people.

During the war her two youngest children were born – Michael in 1916 and John Jacob VII (Jakie) in 1918. Her complete family then consisted of five sons – four of them Astors – and one Astor daughter. The children were looked after by Nannie Gibbons, whom they loved and whom Nancy described as her 'strength and stay' and the 'backbone' of her home. Like most nannies of the period, she was left more or less free to run her own department, but she accepted the implications for her charges of Nancy's conversion to Christian Science.

The Astors' way of life was modified by the war, particularly by the absence of menservants, but all the same it was maintained at a level of reduced luxury rather than austerity. There was still a good deal of entertaining at Cliveden, and also at 4 St James's Square. But just before the war ended the London house was lent to the YMCA as a rest hostel for American officers, and so it remained until the summer of 1919.

Waldorf spent the early part of the war as an army major with the uninspiring task of checking waste in army units in Britain. Then for a time he served as an inspector in ordnance factories. But things looked up for him at the end of 1916, when David Lloyd George became Prime Minister and appointed Waldorf his Parliamentary Private Secretary. Waldorf thus became a member of the famous 'garden suburb' at 10 Downing Street, along with Philip Kerr and others. During the last month of the war he received his first ministerial appointment, as Parliamentary Secretary to the Ministry of Food.

As a protégé of Lloyd George his career was prospering, but by now there was a blight on his future, resulting from an arbitrary act by his father. The New Year

Nannie Gibbons with four of her charges, (left to right) Bill, David, Michael (on lap) and Wissie

Honours' List for 1916 had included a peerage for old William Waldorf Astor, and this meant that Waldorf could stay in the House of Commons for only so long as his father survived. Waldorf and Nancy were outraged by the decision, about which they were not consulted or even informed in advance. According to Nancy, her father-in-law had vowed to her that he would never become a peer, so she felt personally let down. In fact, his decision was to be the making of her career, whatever harm it may have done to Waldorf's.

The Armistice in 1918 was soon followed by a general election, in which for the first time women took part as voters and candidates. This was the all-important change, so far as Nancy was concerned, though she had done little to bring it about and did not at the time dream of standing for Parliament herself.

The change is generally said to have been made 'inevitable' by the demonstration of women's ability to do men's jobs during the war; also to some

Nancy's family complete, in 1918: left to right, Wissie, Jakie (in arms), Nancy, Bobbie,
Michael, David and Bill

extent by the martyrdom of Edith Cavell, which created a profound impression. The militant pre-war campaign by the Women's Social and Political Union – the suffragettes – is given no credit for the change, but is said to have delayed rather than promoted the enfranchisement of women. But is this really true? Prejudice is less often overcome by sentiment than by fear, and the all-male political establishment that conceded votes to women in 1917 (and in 1918 the right of women to stand for Parliament) cannot have relished the prospect of renewed suffragette militancy. Until the Great War brought about a truce in the sex war, the lives of British statesmen were being made a misery by the suffragettes; and the same men knew that the truce would be no more than temporary unless women were given the vote. The other, more dignified reasons for the change were doubtless influential, but not necessarily decisive.

Nancy had always been a strong feminist, but whatever the pros and cons of the suffragette movement, she took no part in it. She was, however, proud of Waldorf for identifying himself openly with the cause of women's suffrage, to the annoyance and disquiet of some Plymouth Conservatives; and she was a secret admirer of the suffragette leaders, Mrs Pankhurst and her formidable daughter, Christabel. In one of her pre-war letters to Phyllis she writes (from Biarritz): 'Mrs Pankhurst is determined to go on. Nothing will stop her. Christabel is in Paris & I am to see her when I go through. I am greatly looking forward to that.' And just after the outbreak of war, which turned the Pankhursts into super-patriots, she reports, after hearing Mrs Pankhurst give a recruiting speech, that she has never heard such a good speaker.

In the general election of December 1918 there were seventeen women candidates, despite the fact that the legislation enabling women to stand received the Royal Assent less than a month before polling day. Among the candidates were some names famous in the suffragette movement, including Mrs Pethick-Lawrence, Mrs Despard and Christabel Pankhurst. All of the women who stood in Great Britain were defeated, though Christabel, at Smethwick, lost by only 775 votes. Unlike nearly half of the candidates, she did not stand on behalf of any of the established parties, but as the candidate of a specifically Women's Party. Without the help of an existing party organization and with the (supposed) disadvantage of her unrivalled record of militancy, she nevertheless came within a very short distance of being the first woman to sit in Parliament. Nothing, however, fails like failure, and her remarkable performance in 1918 is now virtually forgotten.

In Ireland one candidate *was* elected, but was self-disqualified from taking her seat. Constance Gore-Booth, whose married name was Countess Markievicz, was elected as Sinn Fein candidate for the St Patrick's division of Dublin. Her campaign, such as it was, had been conducted from Holloway Gaol (where she was held as a potential rebel), and her election address had been written on a sheet of prison notepaper. After her election she refused, in common with the other Sinn Feiners – who swept the poll in Ireland – to take the oath of allegiance. So she could not become the first woman to sit at Westminster, and for nearly another year that honour was still going begging.

To whom would it fall? The question was entirely open when, in October 1919, William Waldorf, 1st Viscount Astor, died. Few at the time realized that his death might provide an answer to the question, though the *Evening Standard* did report a rumour that the new Conservative candidate at Plymouth, to take the place that Waldorf was now obliged to vacate, would be Nancy.

The rumour was premature. Waldorf's first thought was to find some legal means of averting his removal from the Commons. He had been moved from the Ministry of Food to the Local Government Board and, more recently, to the newly created Ministry of Health, where he was Parliamentary Secretary. Though as a

Campaigning in Plymouth during 1919 by-election, with eloquent backdrop

peer he would not be disqualified from remaining a minister, he felt that his chances of serious advancement would be damaged. In any case, he had no desire to give up his seat or to be wafted into the House of Lords.

There was, however, no legal escape (and none existed until the law was changed more than forty years later). So the Plymouth Conservatives had to look for another candidate to fight the inevitable by-election. Apparently they decided to make an approach to Nancy without any prompting from Waldorf, though it cannot have been absent from his or their thoughts that it might be convenient for his wife to have the seat and to keep it warm for him, in case the law governing the inheritance of peerages were before long to be changed as a result of his efforts.

After some hesitation Nancy agreed to stand. Quite apart from the reason of convenience just mentioned, she had strong claims to be chosen in her own right. During Waldorf's nine years as MP she had concerned herself with Plymouth and its people far beyond the line of duty. Her letters to Phyllis show that her attitude had been less that of a typical MP's wife than that of an exceptionally conscientious and sympathetic MP. Moreover, those who had worked with her most closely knew how good she was at getting across to ordinary people. When the Executive consulted the various ward committees, it was found that support for her was very strong.

She was adopted unanimously, and she stood – like Waldorf the year before – as a Conservative supporter of the Lloyd George Coalition. In her adoption speech she emphasized her Coalitionism rather than her Conservatism. 'If you want a party hack don't elect me. Surely we have outgrown party ties. I have. The war has taught us that there is a greater thing than parties and that is the State.'

Plymouth was no longer the single, two-Member constituency that it had been when Waldorf first got in, but was now divided into three. The part that Nancy had to hold was the Sutton division, containing Sutton Harbour (whence the *Mayflower* set sail for America) and the picturesque but impoverished area of the city known as the Barbican. This was to be her favourite area, both for electioneering and for social work.

In 1918 Waldorf had won with a majority of about 11,750 over Labour, but during the past year the Coalition had been losing by-elections. So the contest could not be regarded as a walkover, quite apart from the imponderable factor of prejudice against a woman candidate. Nancy had to face two opponents, William Gay for Labour and Isaac Foot for the Asquithian Liberals. Gay was a Co-op man with a reputation for pacifism; he had a good organization and had stood at the previous election. Foot was a much-respected local solicitor, Methodist preacher and sage, who had, however, a considerable record of electoral failure in other constituencies.

Nancy took a tough line against Gay, probably because she regarded him as the more serious threat. He represented 'the shirking classes', she said, whereas she represented the working classes. It needed incredible nerve to make such a claim, as a millionairess and a viscountess, but nerve was always a prime ingredient in her political style. Her treatment of Foot was equally cavalier though more amiable. He was a personal friend.

She was never on the defensive, least of all about her wealth. She drove about the constituency in a brightly decorated carriage and pair, with a coachman in livery, and she was always careful to look her best. It was a rule with her never to 'dress down'; in the poorest streets of Plymouth she would be dressed as for a lunch at St James's Square. When somebody shouted: 'You're too rich to get the working men's vote', she replied: 'You'll see. It won't be the seventeen thousand millionaires living on the Hoe who will elect me.'

Since she knew that the poor people of Plymouth had her true measure from long experience of her work among them, she could afford to make the sort of jokes that would have been fatal to any ordinary candidate with her privileges. 'And now, my dears', she ended one speech, 'I'm going back to one of my beautiful palaces to sit down in my tiara and do nothing, and when I roll out in my car I will splash you all with mud and look the other way.' Another time she said: 'Today I heard a thing they are saying about me and must tell you: "We know Lady Astor. She comes among us all smiles and then goes back to her big house and calls her maid: 'Have my gloves cleaned, I've shaken hands with a Tommy.'"' Such remarks, coming from her, were greeted with friendly laughter and loud applause.

One of her helpers in the election was Oswald Mosley, then a young MP on

Tackling the Royal Navy: Sir Oswald Mosley (centre) looking out of the car window

the left wing of the Conservative Party, and soon to be married to Lord Curzon's daughter Cynthia, of whom Nancy was very fond. Speaking recently of the campaign, he recalled her 'direct approach':

She had, of course, unlimited effrontery. She was less shy than any woman – or any man – one has ever known. She'd address the audience and then she'd go across to some old woman scowling in a neighbouring doorway, who simply hated her, take both her hands and kiss her on the cheek or something of that sort. She was absolutely unabashed by any situation. Great effrontery but also, of course, enormous charm. People were usually overcome by it. She was much better when she was interrupted. She must have prayed for hecklers and interrupters. She certainly got a lot.

Nancy did indeed realize how necessary heckling was to her. 'It takes opponents to get me gingered up,' she said during the by-election – and this was also her attitude in private life. (In one of her pre-war letters to Phyllis she complains of the excessive politeness of Waldorf's, sister, Pauline. 'I can't get any forrader [*sic*] with her. Such sweetness absolutely cramps my style.') When a coal-heaver challenged her to say what Waldorf had ever done for the likes of him, she shouted back: 'Charlie, you old liar, you know quite well what he has done' – and then posed with Charlie for a photograph. Passing the driver of a petrol lorry, she asked him if he was going to vote for her. But seeing that he was smoking, she quickly added: 'If you don't put out that cigarette you won't vote for anybody.'

Obviously she was a gift to reporters and there were droves of them covering the campaign. The eyes of the world were upon her, and more especially the eyes of the United States. Americans were fascinated by the Sutton election not only because of Nancy's origins, but because the issue of votes for women was topical in their country. In June 1919 it had been proposed that the US Constitution should be amended so that the right of citizens to vote should 'not be denied or abridged on account of sex'. What became the Nineteenth Amendment was eventually passed in August of the following year, when the necessary three-fourths of the States ratified it. Five Southern States did not ratify, but Nancy must have been pleased to note that Virginia was not one of them.

Polling in Sutton was on 15 November, but the count had to be delayed until the 28th, because the votes of men serving overseas had to be brought in. During the interlude Waldorf tried to get a motion passed by his friends and supporters in the House of Commons, enabling a bill to be introduced legitimizing the surrender of peerages. But the motion was defeated by a large majority, so it was clear that if Nancy were elected she would not sit in Parliament merely as a temporary proxy for her husband.

The 28 November was a very cold day in Plymouth, with ice on the ground and occasional flurries of snow. The count lasted until mid-afternoon, but

After declaration of the poll, 1919 – Liberal opponent Isaac Foot (extreme right), Labour opponent William Gay (left, with hand to mouth)

then the candidates emerged from the Guildhall to hear the Town Clerk declare the result to the waiting crowd, which, despite the weather, was very large. Nancy had polled more than the other two candidates combined and was in with a majority of more than five thousand. At the previous election Waldorf's majority had been more than twice as big, but the circumstances then were exceptionally favourable. In the altered circumstances of late 1919 Nancy's result was, on the whole, a satisfactory one. In any case it made history.

After the declaration the candidates' speeches were scarcely audible amid the hubbub. Then Nancy's carriage was drawn to the Conservative Club by a group of enthusiasts, including sailors, and from the balcony of the Club she made a short speech, which ended: 'I ought to feel sorry for Mr Foot and Mr Gay, but I don't. The only man I feel sorry for is the poor old Viscount here.'

Next day she returned to Cliveden, and while changing trains at Paddington was greeted by, among others, veteran suffragettes, who must have reflected wryly on the strange workings of Providence, that Nancy of all women should have been chosen as the realization of their dream. One of them presented her with a badge and touched her by saying: 'It is the beginning of our era. I am glad I have suffered for this.' But, as usual with Nancy, the scene was marked by comedy as well as emotion. A rough-looking man shouted: 'I never voted for you', to which Nancy promptly replied: 'Thank Heaven for that!'

[77]

OVERLEAF *Triumphal ride, after the declaration of the poll: the carriage being drawn to the Conservative Club by exultant supporters*

At Cliveden bonfires were lit, and she and Waldorf had to get out of their car at the gates, so that tenants and estate workers could draw them in an old Victoria along the drive to the front door of the house. Then she had one day to recover before the ceremony of taking her seat.

On 1 December after Question Time she was introduced into the House of Commons, wearing the black coat and skirt, white blouse and black hat that were to be her Parliamentary uniform (though the hat was not yet of the tricorn variety that she later adopted). *Punch* described her as 'demurely but daintily garbed', and one of the Clerks thought her appearance 'suggestive of Shakespeare's Portia, fair-minded and fastidious and a little didactic'. So far as he was concerned appearances were, it must be said, partially misleading, because fair-mindedness was never one of Nancy's more obvious qualities.

Bobbie alone of her children was able to accompany her to Westminster and witness the great occasion. Her Astor children were either at school or in the nursery. The two MPs who introduced her were Lloyd George and Arthur Balfour. This was appropriate not only because they were the only Members of prime ministerial rank (one the actual, the other a previous, Prime Minister), but also because they both had a long record of support for the women's cause. Lloyd George seems to have slightly bungled his part in the ceremony, but Nancy's performance was generally admired – though some purists were a little disconcerted when she talked to friends on the Front Bench after taking the oath but before signing the Roll. Had they known her better, and as they were soon to know her, they would have realized that for such a compulsive chatterbox she was abnormally self-controlled.

Some years later she re-enacted the scene in a film documentary, with all the roles apart from her own played by actors. The film gives, presumably, an authentic impression of her own speech and bearing on the day, but – to judge from other accounts – it seems to exaggerate the enthusiasm of her reception. In fact, she was received in a courteous, even ostensibly sympathetic, spirit, but without any undue demonstrativeness. If Members had shown their true feelings there might have been plenty of noise, though not all of it of an enthusiastic kind.

Whatever they felt, she was there. Lady Astor MP was a fact. Britain's ancient Parliament would never be the same again.

Chillie Langhorne did not live to see his daughter a world figure. He had died the previous February. In his will he left each of his children, including Nancy, an income of ten thousand dollars a year. But she let this income accumulate in a separate account, because, as she put it, she had not married an Astor to spend her own money.

Nancy arriving to take her seat in Parliament, 1 December 1919, with the men surrounding her seeming to caricature themselves

5

Women
and Children First

Sca

IT could be said that the most important political achievement of Nancy's career was already behind her when she went to bed on 1 December 1919; that, having performed the historic task of showing that a woman could enter the House of Commons, the rest of her activity there during the twenty-five years of her membership was relatively trifling. This could be said – but it would not be true.

It was not enough for a woman to be elected and to take her seat. If the cause of women was to prevail, it was no less essential that she should impose upon the six-hundred-year-old men's club both her own personality and the personality, as it were, of her sex. Nancy had to ensure that her Parliamentary colleagues would never for one moment forget that there was a woman in their midst – a 'stranger in the House' who could not, however, like other strangers, be evicted.

She had to avoid at all costs being assimilated and so becoming, in effect, an honorary man. Old institutions have a powerful atmosphere which can force groups of newcomers, let alone isolated individuals, to conform. And in 1919 it was commonly believed that women were the weaker sex, whose function in the natural order was to accept the leadership of men. For nearly two years Nancy was the only woman in the House of Commons. But she did not conform; she was not assimilated.

Perhaps she was the ideal woman for the task, with her unique blend of femininity and masculinity, of frivolity and seriousness, of delicacy and earthiness. To do what she did required an overweening independence of spirit, and this she undoubtedly had. It was inherent in her character, but also, of course, much assisted by her beauty, wit and wealth.

The sum of her assets was not possessed by any other political woman of her time. Certainly it was not possessed by those who had been in the forefront of the

[83]

OPPOSITE ABOVE *With a young evacuee at Taplow Lodge, October 1939*
BELOW *One resistant to Nancy's charm*

struggle for women's rights, or by public-spirited female intellectuals of the Beatrice Webb type. Such women would either have succumbed to the mystique and mumbo-jumbo of Parliament or would have resisted it in such a way as to bore and antagonize the public outside. Nancy's capital achievement was to defy the conventions without forfeiting, indeed while enhancing, a popularity that was by no means confined to her own sex. Mary Stocks put it well in an essay on Nancy, written much later:

At first sight it almost seemed that Lady Glencora Palliser had come blazing out of the pages of Anthony Trollope, pushed her way through half a century of time, and taken headlong possession of the seat vacated by a newly ennobled Duke of Omnium. Like Lady Glencora, Lady Astor was a positive personality – there could be no doubt of that. But could one trust her discretion? Clearly one could not. And yet from the first moment of her appearance in that exclusive club a terrifying responsibility rested upon her. She carried the repute of future women MPs in her elegant gloved hands . . . . Everybody waited to see what she would say or do; and those who resented female incursion into that sacred male preserve devoutly prayed that she might say or do the wrong thing.

She did not say or do the wrong thing, but she often said and did the unexpected thing.

Whether wrong or unexpected, what she said in Parliament was more often than not out of order. As Lord Campion, an expert observer, has written: 'She would keep up a running and very audible commentary on a speech with which she disagreed, or continue to interrupt when the Member speaking refused to give way.' She never attempted to cultivate a Parliamentary manner, but brought her own manner, with all its sparkle and directness, into the House of Commons. Harold Nicolson, who was in the House with her, paid her this tribute in an unpublished essay:

Her courage . . . was such that no subsequent woman Member ever felt inferiority when faced with that predominantly male assembly. It was Lady Astor who, from the very day of her introduction, taught her contemporaries that the expansion of woman's liberty could be achieved, not by mute acquiescence, but by voluble pugnacity. She taught her sex to fight. [And] in a Parliament composed of men of very different origins, her utter lack of class-consciousness, her merry mixing ways, proved a wonderful solvent of stiffness or embarrassment. She made no distinction at all between Prime Ministers or back-bench mutes, between Conservative magnates or young Socialists from South Wales; to her friendly banter they all fell victims and although her chaff often irritated, and occasionally wounded, it was directed impartially to all sides.

One of her bugbears was the Conservative magnate, Sir Frederick Banbury, who strongly disapproved of her. When interruption failed she tried, on one occasion, to stop him speaking by pulling him down by his coat-tails. Another

Having it out with a floating voter? Another glimpse of Nancy in 1929 election

with whom she frequently clashed was the Labour MP for Silvertown, Jack Jones (not to be confused with the recent General Secretary of the TGWU), who spent much of his time in the House of Commons bar and was often the worse for wear. One day when Nancy was speaking, he came back into the Chamber to interrupt her. She told him in return that he was drinking too much and should think of the effect upon his stomach; to which he replied that he would put his stomach up against hers any time she liked. A witness reports that this gross jest was greeted with loud guffaws – not very nice for the solitary woman MP. But Nancy could take it.

A large number of her colleagues found her presence objectionable in principle, and even more objectionable because of her way of making it felt. Conspicuous among the objectors was Winston Churchill, who had never really favoured women's suffrage and whose mode of speaking was particularly uncongenial to Nancy, as her mode of interruption was to him.

The Churchills had been quite close friends of the Astors before the war (despite Nancy's initially contemptuous view of Clemmie, quoted earlier), but after Nancy became an MP the relationship cooled and in the 1930s it was further impaired by profound disagreements over Imperial and foreign policy. Above all, there was a conflict of temperaments. Churchill was a man of genius who, unlike Lloyd George (with whom Nancy always got on very well), had an addiction to monologue and was a bad listener. Nancy was incapable of treating anybody with the reverence that Churchill felt to be his due. She said that he united 'the worst blood of two continents', and no doubt the remark was repeated to him.

Apart from her dramatic success in keeping her end up as the lone pioneer of womanhood at Westminster, Nancy also achieved positive results in the field of work where she felt she had a special responsibility. Without regarding herself as exclusively a representative of women's interests, she did feel that, as the only woman MP, she was better qualified than all her male colleagues to defend the interests of the home. 'Women and children first' might have been her motto as a Parliamentarian, for it was in that spirit that most of her work – and certainly her best work – was done.

Her maiden speech was a plea for State control of drink, on the lines of the 'Carlisle experiment' that had been introduced during the Great War. She spoke with earnestness, but without undue passion.

I do not want you to look on your lady Member as a fanatic or lunatic. I am simply trying to speak for hundreds of women and children throughout the country who cannot speak for themselves. I want to tell you that I do know the working man, and I know that, if you tell him the truth about drink, he would be as willing as anybody else to put up with these vexatious restrictions.

Though most Members disagreed with her, the speech went down well.

During the by-election her views on drink had been an issue, because Prohibition had recently been brought in in the United States and she was suspected of being a Prohibitionist. She explained, however, that her policy was not to ban drink completely, but rather to control and restrict its sale. As MP for a gin-manufacturing port city it was a risky line to take, and at the next general election she had to face the challenge of a rival Conservative candidate. But she survived the challenge. Moreover in 1923 she succeeded in getting a piece of restrictive legislation through. This was the Intoxicating Liquor (Sale to Persons under Eighteen) Act, which limited the availability of drink to teenagers. As amended, it made the sale of drink 'knowingly' to persons under eighteen illegal in principle, though young people between fourteen and eighteen were still free to consume wine, beer or cider with a meal in a public house or restaurant. Nancy piloted the measure through the House of Commons as a private Member's bill, and Waldorf looked after it in the Lords.

In one of her speeches on Temperance she showed that the mistress of Cliveden, Rest Harrow, 4 St James's Square and 3 Elliot Terrace had not forgotten her early childhood in Danville. 'People who live in two houses do not realise what it is like to live in two rooms. That's what is wrong with the Conservatives.' Though she now lived in four houses, she could remember living in four rooms.

In 1931 she went too far when she claimed that the Australian cricketers had regained the Ashes because they did not drink. This remark was regarded as defamatory by the Australians no less than by the English.

Another domestic subject on which she took a strong line, though it exposed her to worse obloquy, was divorce. When, in 1920, there was a move to extend the grounds for divorce beyond adultery, Nancy opposed it.

The spiritual idea of marriage, though started in the East, has been more highly developed in the West, and it is that that has elevated the Western women a little above their Eastern sisters. . . . We must do nothing which will weaken it. . . . I am not convinced that making divorce very easy really makes marriages more happy or makes happy marriages more possible.

The argument was perfectly consistent with her own matrimonial record, because she had refused to obtain a divorce from her first husband on the easy American ground of incompatibility, but had insisted that it must be on account of his adultery. All the same, divorce was obviously an awkward subject for her, and a less courageous woman would have steered clear of it. At the by-election she was able to dispose of it lightly. When a woman asked if she favoured a reform of the divorce law, she merely remarked: 'Madam, I am sorry to hear you are in trouble.'

But in 1920 she came under attack from the crook and demagogue, Horatio

Horatio Bottomley with associates arriving at Bow Street, October 1921

Bottomley, who accused her of gross hypocrisy in his paper *John Bull*. The charge was made to seem more plausible by the fact that Waldorf had described her in *Who's Who* as the 'widow' of Robert Gould Shaw. Fortunately her stock was so high that public and Parliamentary opinion supported her against Bottomley, whose fraudulent career was anyway nearing its end. (He was convicted and sent to prison in 1922.)

In October 1921 Nancy was joined by another woman Member, Mrs Wintringham, who also was returned at a by-election in succession to her husband, though in her case as a result of his death. She sat as a Liberal. At the 1923 general election eight women were returned, including three representing Labour. One of these was Margaret Bondfield, who in 1929 became the first woman Cabinet minister. Nancy acted as a mother-hen to the new women MPs, regardless of party. Mrs Wintringham, for instance, became a frequent visitor to Cliveden, and a particularly warm friendship developed between Nancy and a famous Labour woman MP elected in 1924, Ellen Wilkinson. Of course not all of Nancy's female colleagues liked her, but all had reason to be grateful for her pioneering effort and example.

Outside Parliament, too, she showed a maternal sense of responsibility towards the large and confused 'family' of women's movements. On 1 March 1921

Group of women MPs, October 1924: left to right, Dorothy Jewson, Susan Lawrence, Nancy, Mrs Wintringham, Duchess of Atholl, Mrs Philipson, Lady Terrington, Margaret Bondfield

a conference of women representing more than forty of them was held, on her initiative, at 4 St James's Square. Among the bodies represented were the International Woman Suffrage Alliance, the Central Committee for Women's Employment, the National Union of Women Teachers, the College of Nursing, the Society for the Prevention of Cruelty to Children and the National Council for the Unmarried Mother. In a brief opening speech Nancy said that one year's experience in the House of Commons had helped her to see certain ways in which the pressure of women's organizations on Parliament lacked effectiveness. She suggested that there might be a 'headquarters organization' to give their work a more concerted impact, and said that if she could be of any further use to them she would be only too glad.

By the middle of the year a Consultative Committee of Women's Organizations had come into being. Its object was to improve the political, economic and social status of women. In a memorandum on its work Nancy mentioned a number of themes in which she herself would take a very active interest: women police (who should be regarded as a necessity not a 'superfluous luxury'), slum clearance, new and better housing, open spaces for recreation, day nurseries, clinics and play centres.

[91]

OPPOSITE *Nancy with the second woman MP. Mrs Wintringham, on the terrace of the House of Commons, 1922*

Nancy with a visibly shy David at the Wellington, Canning Town, 1924: eating 'bangers and mash'

Nancy's capacity to give a practical lead to women was, of course, made easier by the hospitality that she was able to dispense and by the secretarial resources that she commanded. The meetings at St James's Square were not like meetings in some dreary public place, and during the early days of the Consultative Committee Nancy's political secretary, Hilda Matheson, acted as its honorary secretary. (In due course it acquired a paid secretary of its own.) After the second of Nancy's preparatory conferences, she received this letter from Eleanor Rathbone, a leading campaigner for women's rights and, later, an outstanding Independent MP:

Dear Lady Astor,

I feel I must thank you personally for all the trouble you took about yesterday's conference – and for having us at all, and entertaining us so royally, at a time when your mind must be full of other things.

Miss Matheson organized it splendidly and I think it has given us a real lift forward towards better cooperation.

It's such a comfort to feel that the one woman MP is someone who really cares about women's questions and has the pluck to stand up for unpopular causes. But will you forgive me for saying that 'the one woman MP' looks as though she ought to go on strike & have at least a month's holiday.

Sincerely yours
Eleanor F. Rathbone.

It was not long before the Astors launched their own schemes of social betterment in Plymouth. In 1925, after a year of negotiations with the local

OPPOSITE *Ellen Wilkinson with a policeman outside the House of Commons* authority, the Lady Astor Housing Trust was set up. Its aim was to provide 'model dwellings for the working classes' in the city. According to *Time and Tide*, it was 'of special interest to housing reformers', because it had several novel features. One of these was that three-quarters of the tenants were to be families with young children, and there were to be rent reductions for each child under fourteen. In addition, two recreational centres were established by the Astors in Plymouth – the Astor Institute and the Virginia House Settlement. The second of these was Nancy's favourite, because it was near the Barbican and its membership, which soon exceeded a thousand, was largely drawn from that area. The Settlement was housed in converted factory buildings, and its facilities included clubrooms, libraries, a cinema, a gymnasium, a carpenter's shop and a printing press (where the Settlement's own fixture cards etc. were produced). There were also outdoor activities such as football, boating and camping.

Nancy regarded Plymouth as, in a sense, home and therefore felt that her charity should begin there – an attitude which could easily be misunderstood by political opponents. But her philanthropic efforts were by no means confined to her own constituency. Her response to distress and deprivation was nation-wide.

Immediately after the General Strike in 1926 she and Mrs Wintringham spent two days in the valleys of South Wales and were horrified by what they saw. As Nancy said in a broadcast, they had always tried 'to put the welfare of children first, and above party'; so they went to see for themselves. They found 'no actual starvation and heard of none', but they did observe 'conditions . . . bound to lead to under-nourishment and real suffering very soon' if the miners' families were not helped. Nancy was broadcasting on behalf of the Save the Children Fund, which had been started just after the Great War, and which was now raising money specially for the mining districts. The tone of her appeal may have irritated some Socialists and hard-line Conservatives, and could, perhaps, be described as rather naïve. But who could doubt its sincerity?

We found such kindness and courage, and no bitterness among the miners and their wives. . . . We returned with a longing to help, not only with milk and food, but in bringing about some method of settling disputes by some other way than war – for industrial disputes are war, in which the women and children suffer first and most. It all seems so useless and hopeless – here in this country, where all sections of the community seem to have the same virtues and the same faults. They certainly have the same sporting instincts, for they all asked for the winner of the Derby, and got a lecture on the evils of betting for their pains!

Please send your gifts. . . . Remember that by doing this you will help to keep alive not only the bodies and spirits of those who are suffering, but, what is more important, their faith in their fellow men and women.

Another cause that Nancy enthusiastically espoused, from the mid-1920s

Recording a message in the early 1920s

onwards, was that of providing more recreational space for children. She was one of the founders of the National Playing Fields Association, and at a meeting to launch it in the Albert Hall her speech delighted the audience, which had been made restless by a succession of pompous and boring speakers before her.

I can speak with a full heart on the subject of playing fields, for no one ever loved playing games – or just playing – more than I did and, alas, do. And half the trouble we are up against is that some grown-ups forget how to play.

To me there is no more tragic figure than the small boy or girl taken up for playing in the streets. He may be fined, but it is we grown-ups who should be convicted and condemned.

She made a special plea for girls:

There is an old notion that girls ought to be always at home darning stockings and cooking meals. . . . Of course, there is a right thought at the back of this old idea. I am all for women and girls knowing about housework – they are the first to suffer if they don't. But good housekeeping nowadays demands an iron constitution, and an iron constitution demands fresh air and exercise.

There was always a tug-of-war in Nancy between her genuine feminism and her no less genuine reluctance to say goodbye to the traditional role of women. This was particularly noticeable in her demands for wider job opportunities for women, which were often accompanied, incongruously, by rhapsodies on the beauty of home life. She seems never to have reconciled her desire for equality of the sexes with her sense that a wife and mother should be more or less constantly present in any home worth the name. And no wonder, because the two things are, in fact, incompatible.

For working mothers who could not leave their children for most of the time

[95]

in the care of nannies, as she could, the only answer was the nursery school. Nancy was able to give whole-hearted support to nursery schools, because she saw that they were good not only for mothers who wanted or needed to work, but also for children with squalid and inadequate home backgrounds. The pioneer of nursery schools (and, incidentally, of the medical inspection of schoolchildren) was Margaret McMillan, whose family came from the Inverness area and who was herself educated there, though born in the United States. With her sister Rachel, Margaret McMillan founded the first nursery school in Deptford during the Great War, and the experiment aroused emulous interest not only in other parts of Britain but in many foreign countries as well. When Rachel died in 1917, Margaret carried on the work with a mystical belief that they were still doing it together.

In 1926 she and Nancy became friends and the friendship became, as well, a working partnership. Margaret's efforts were already recognized and admired before Nancy entered her life, but Nancy brought a new injection of prestige and, of course, money. She enjoyed visiting the children at Deptford, and they enjoyed her visits. At the same time she brightened Margaret's last years and won her passionate devotion.

In one of her first letters to Nancy she writes: 'I read everything I can about you; and I think you are perhaps like Giotto's Charity who stood on riches, because she was accepting Heaven's gift of a heart.' And not long afterwards: 'I was reading Lord Shaftesbury's Life yesterday, & I think you are in the succession of those who are to destroy the Drink Traffic. It makes havoc of child-life, & I don't know how or why it is permitted.'

Lady Astor Housing Trust estate, Mount Gold, Plymouth 1927

One letter in 1929 contains an odd simile, in view of the writer's and recipient's views on drink.

Dearest, kindest, sweetest Nancy in the world!
You haven't the least notion what a friend & ally to the death you've made of me. My love for you is all mixed up with my love for the children & I don't feel I can get old or die or anything while you are singing in my veins like wine.

Later in the same year Nancy had good reason to appreciate what a friend and ally she had made of Margaret McMillan. During the 1929 election Margaret, though a long-time adherent of the ILP, spoke for her friend at Plymouth – where, of course, a McMillan nursery school had been established. Since Nancy held her seat that year with a majority of only 211, the intervention on her side of a famous, if unorthodox, Labour figure may have made all the difference. Perhaps Margaret was less of a Socialist than she seemed, because two years before she had written to Nancy: 'What a smack you are giving the Labour Party. *Mercy*! What a *smack* ... Well! We always loved America.' Ardent Socialists were apt to regard her work

Margaret McMillan (third from right) with Queen Mary, after the opening of Rachel McMillan Training College, Deptford, 8 May 1930

Nancy (towards left of picture) at the opening of a nursery school at Wrotham, May 1936; the Duke of York, soon afterwards George VI, between mayors

as no more than tinkering with social evils for the ultimate benefit of capitalism, and from their point of view they may have been right. In fact her motivation, like Nancy's, was primarily religious.

Nancy was full of Christian aspiration, as well as sheer kind-heartedness (which is more dependable than any religious commitment). But she was also very rich, and this tended to distort her view on economic issues. When, in 1930, the Labour Chancellor of the Exchequer, Philip Snowden, had raised income tax from four shillings to four shillings and sixpence in the pound, and also raised surtax so that it would yield an additional twelve and a half million pounds, Nancy wrote to Margaret McMillan (after telling her of a party of East Enders she had been entertaining at Cliveden): 'I am feeling very bitter towards Snowden and his budget, because all the money that we had to give away has been taken, and it means that we shall have to get rid of some of the people off this place, or stop helping the people to whom we have been able to lend a hand.' Such preposterous statements were not uncommon after Lloyd George's budget in 1909, when surtax was first introduced. Nancy was placing herself in an absurd tradition. Of course she did not sack any of her servants, or cut any of her charitable donations, but her hostility to Socialism was, and remained, somewhat exaggerated.

With her flair for language, she managed to hit upon an epigram that made Socialism the antithesis of Christianity. 'Christianity', she told Tom Jones at lunch one day in 1930, 'is discontent with oneself. Socialism is discontent with other people.' But it was hard for her, as a millionairess, to be objective in such a matter, and in any case her own discontent on behalf of other people must have seemed socialistic to some more right-wing Conservatives.

With General Evangeline Booth, Salvation Army, 1937. When Nancy later met General Montgomery he said, 'Lady Astor, I must tell you I don't approve of women politicians', to which she replied, 'That's all right, the only general I approve of is Evangeline Booth'

View of Cliveden, from the south lawn

6

Camelot-on-Thames

❧

NANCY was as much the politician at home as she was her private self in
Parliament. She did not retire to the country at weekends to get away
from political activity, but to carry it on by other means; or rather, by the
same means in a more agreeable setting.

Cliveden and the House of Commons – Barry's classical palazzo at Taplow
and his Gothic palace at Westminster – were of just about equal importance in her
public life. She needed them both; neither would have been anything like as useful
to her, or to the causes she took up, without the other. Her son Jakie (who was in
Parliament for a time, but disliked it) describes the Palace of Westminster as like a
liner in which the Members are passengers, but passengers without cabins. And
Nancy's niece, Joyce Grenfell, used the same image, with a difference, to describe Cliveden. It was, she said, like a great liner, but when Nancy was not
there it seemed that the liner's engines had been turned off.

While she was the only woman Member Nancy did, in fact, have a 'cabin' at
Westminster. Until others joined her in the House she was the sole user of the
boudoir provided for women MPs. But of course she had to compete against many
disadvantages in the House of Commons, where the atmosphere was alien and, in
many ways, hostile. At Cliveden, however, everything was on her side and at her
service. In *that* house she was more than a Speaker, more than a Prime Minister;
she was queen.

The political weekend was still a going concern in the 1920s and 1930s.
People who were involved in politics, and who had large country houses, were
able to entertain assorted men of power and their wives from Friday to Monday,
under conditions that made for free and relaxed talk without fear of exposure. This
is not to say that there was anything sinister about such gatherings. For the most
part they were entirely innocuous, even marginally beneficial, and the fact that
they were private did not mean that they were against the public interest.

Cliveden was an exceptionally convenient place for political house parties,
because it was so close to London. Indeed, in the Astors' day it was really no longer

Family group at Cliveden: front row, left to right, 'Winkie' Brooks (son of Phyllis by her first marriage) and Tommy Phipps (son of Nora); back row, left to right, Joyce Phipps (later Grenfell), Wissie, Irene, Nora and Irene's daughter, 'Babs'

The Astors and children on the terrace at Cliveden, early 1920s: left to right, Michael, Jakie, Nancy, Wissie, Waldorf, David and Bill

Page of the Cliveden visitors' book. New Year 1928, including the signatures of Mr and Mrs George Bernard Shaw. During this visit Bernard Shaw worked on The Apple Cart

a country house at all, but a glorified villa in what has since come to be known as subtopia. The lovely woods that surrounded it, and the deceptively rural landscape across the river, as seen from the terrace, created an illusion of remoteness from city life. But in fact Cliveden was just the largest and grandest unit in a garden-city zone. Guests could leave central London, by train or car, after a full day's work, and reach Cliveden in plenty of time to change for dinner.

The house itself had the feeling more of a country club than a typical country house of the period. This was due, above all, to the composition of the house parties and to the way guests were received. The clientèle at Cliveden was far more diverse than in any other comparable place. It was not simply a mixture of family, close friends and political associates. There would also be a fair sprinkling of people who were unknown to each other, their fellow-guests and the world at large, and who might also have only a slight acquaintance with their hosts.

On arrival visitors were received not by Nancy or Waldorf, but by the butler,

Mr Edwin Lee, or by a footman. Inside the hall there was a list of guests and the rooms allotted to them. The new arrivals checked in and were shown to their rooms, as in a hotel. Then they had to fend for themselves. If they knew the place and its denizens already, they were soon comfortably in the swim. But if they were newcomers, the first few hours might be disconcerting, even alarming, for them. When in due course they ran into Nancy or Waldorf they would be welcomed, but very likely not introduced to others present. This might spare them immediate embarrassment, but left them under the necessity to introduce themselves piecemeal as the weekend proceeded. They must have felt like people staying for the first time in a hotel and trying to get on terms with the 'regulars'.

Somehow it all worked out – more or less. The company at Cliveden reflected the Astors', and more especially Nancy's, many-sidedness, Her own family was always much in evidence: her children and their friends, her sisters and their husbands, her sister's children and (in Lizzie's case) grandchildren. There was also a nucleus of close friends who came very often to Cliveden, and who constituted a sort of 'extended family'. Then there were distinguished strangers – foreign royalty, itinerant American Congressmen or tycoons, celebrities of all kinds invited because they were celebrities. Finally, there were the humble do-gooders, Christian Science practitioners, constituency workers and other non-celebrities, who represented Nancy's missionary side.

Mixed-up herself, she did not shrink from bringing together all the different aspects of her personality in the form of house parties that were, on any rational

Mr Edwin Lee (seated, right) and his team of footmen at Cliveden

view, doomed to fail, but which her genius enabled to succeed. Because she enjoyed life, her guests were happy; because she took life seriously, they were prepared to raise their normal threshold for boredom. Staying at Cliveden was partly a luxurious holiday, partly a seminar or retreat. As such it was a unique experience.

Luxury took the form of excellent meals and excellent drink with the meals, though there was a certain absence of drink before and after. There were outdoor games to be played, acres of garden, lawns and woods for walking, and the river for boating or swimming. The house was very comfortable, with masses of flowers brightening the rooms, and in winter many fires.

Part of Cliveden's charm was its friendly and attentive staff, who had a gruelling job to maintain the high degree of comfort, because Nancy and Waldorf never modernized the house *à l'Américaine*. On the contrary, it remained old-fashioned even by British standards. No guest's bedroom had a washbasin with running water, so hot water in cans had to be carried to the rooms every morning. There was no lift, so all movement and portage from the basement to the top of the house had to be by way of the stairs. Coal for all the bedroom fires had to be humped up by the 'odd men', and the ash brought down in buckets by the

Mr Lee (right) with a footman on the steps of 4 St James's Square

housemaids. It was upstairs, downstairs with a vengeance. (Incidentally, Cliveden consumed a hundred tons of coal every year.)

Even vacuum cleaners made a late appearance at Cliveden. The domestic economy of the place was labour-intensive. But on the whole the Astors kept their servants. The work was hard, but one way and another it seemed worthwhile.

Waldorf had little to do with running the indoor life of Cliveden or of his other houses. That side of things was run by Nancy in collusion with Mr Lee. Their relationship was fruitful, though sometimes tense. Edwin Lee had entered the Astors' service as a footman in 1912, wearing livery with yellow silk stockings, knee breeches and buckled shoes every night, and powdering his hair if there were more than eight for dinner. When the Great War broke out he joined the army and served for most of the time in France, rising to the rank of company-sergeant-major. With his efficiency and natural authority, it is hard to believe that he could not just as well have commanded a battalion. In 1919 he returned to the Astors as Waldorf's valet, but after Nancy's by-election – during which he was at Plymouth throughout, receiving a gold watch from her as a memento – he became the butler and house steward, which he remained until the Astors' connection with Cliveden ended, sadly, in the 1960s. He was with Nancy until Waldorf's death, and thereafter stayed on at Cliveden with their son, Bill.

Why he and Nancy got on is best explained in his own words:

Lady Astor and I had many battles, but she would always give and take; more often she would give than take. But she was very likeable in many ways and one never felt that you were 'an underdog' or anything like it. One minute she would make you feel that you could nearly kill her, but the next time you saw her you would have forgotten all about it and she would be full of fun and life, and like as if she was one's own sister.

When Rosina Harrison came to Cliveden in 1928 – first as Wissie's maid, but soon to be Nancy's – Mr Lee gave her a character-sketch of the mistress of the house. 'She is not a lady as you would understand a lady, Miss Harrison,' he said. 'You won't find her easy'. Rose, as she was always known, certainly did not find Nancy easy. But she stayed with Nancy until her death, and in the autobiography that she published in 1975 her deep affection shines through all the detailed accounts of quarrelling and mutual insolence.

Rose is a tough Yorkshirewoman, who shared Nancy's taste for plain speech and was not daunted by her domineering ways. Like Mr Lee, she could sense the underlying *camaraderie* and was touched by Nancy's genuine concern for ordinary people.

She was an exception to the rule; many mistresses didn't think that servants had parents, let alone brothers and sisters. Of course her attitude affected my work. To have someone putting pleasure in my mother's way, who got so little out of life at the time, gave me the

Rose Harrison (right) dining at the Hotel Astor, New York, March 1953, with stewardess and hairdresser from a transatlantic liner. Nancy had given them an evening out, including a performance of South Pacific

incentive to try twice as hard. But I don't want anyone to think that that was the reason for her ladyship's kindness. She gave without any thought of return.

Some, by contrast, have described Nancy as 'an Indian giver', or one who expected a return on her generosity. But Rose's view, based on long and intimate observation, must stand as a very good testimonial. For nearly forty years she was as close to Nancy as anybody. Though outwardly mistress and servant, they were sisters under the skin.

Nancy's relations with her actual family will be discussed in the next chapter, but mention has been made of her 'extended family' and some attempt should now be made to define this, though in reality it defies definition. Mr Lee, Rose and a few other employees unquestionably belonged to it, and so did a number of Nancy's special friends, male and female. If there was a 'Cliveden Set' it was not, as later suggested, a political cabal at a specific time and for a specific object, but a group of public-spirited friends whose presence at Cliveden was frequent and natural. United in affection for the Astors, and for each other, they became an accepted part of the place.

The main component of Nancy's 'extended family' was the Round Table group. Several of its members had been friends of Waldorf's at New College, Oxford, and had then served in Milner's 'Kindergarten' in South Africa. On their return they founded a quarterly magazine, *The Round Table*, and formed a group, to which others were recruited, to propagate their ideas and ideals. They believed in the British Empire, the English-speaking world and social reform. They were high-minded but, in most cases, not at all lacking in humour.

When Nancy married Waldorf she, in a sense, married his friends as well. If to the Round Table group Waldorf was a benevolent King Arthur, Nancy was an inspiring, though strictly virtuous, Guinevere. And Cliveden became the group's Camelot. (The romantic analogy may seem more appropriate in this context than when applied to John F. Kennedy, Jacqueline Onassis and the White House during the Kennedy era.) The founder members of the group were Philip Kerr, R.H. Brand, Lionel Curtis, Geoffrey Dawson (or Robinson as he was called until 1917), Lionel Hichens and Dougal Malcolm. An early recruit was another Milnerite, Edward Grigg, and close associates of the Round Table, also very often at Cliveden, were John Buchan, Basil Blackwood, F.S. Oliver and J.L. Garvin, editor of Waldorf's paper, *The Observer*.

Philip Kerr's special relationship with the Astors has already been noted, but in varying degrees other members of the group became similarly attached. R.H. Brand became an actual member of the family when he later married Nancy's sister, Phyllis, after a long courtship. Of Nancy's effect upon himself and other members of the 'Kindergarten', he has written in an unpublished essay:

We were earnest unsophisticated young men, who had lived very hard-working bachelor lives for years. . . . There were only about fifty women to every hundred men in Johannesburg and even when there were women in the circles among which we moved not many of them were unmarried or as young as we were. We had certainly never met anyone like Nancy. . . . There was such a startling combination of great beauty, extreme frankness and friendliness, brilliant wit, tremendous energy and dashing initiative. We supposed you might find some combination of these qualities, or some of them, in the 'fast set'. But yet in her case all this was combined with deep religious and moral principles.

Guinevere, yes – or even a sort of 'Virgin Queen', Gloriana: that was Nancy's status in the eyes of her chivalrous courtiers. Perhaps coincidentally, many of them tended either not to marry, like Philip Kerr, or to marry late. Nancy for her part liked to have them around and relished their admiration, because she felt that they were an élite with enlightened, disinterested views. While they were dazzled by her, in a way she was also dazzled by them, because she always had a high respect for intellectuals. She used to say half-seriously that she had one virtue, seeking and appreciating the company of her betters.

Throughout the inter-war years Cliveden provided a collective home for the Round Table group. Though of course they had, as individuals, many other spheres of activity, they came to Cliveden, like the moon and stars in *The Ancient Mariner*, as to 'their own natural homes, which they enter unannounced, as lords that are certainly expected and yet there is a silent joy at their arrival'.

In most cases marriage did not sever, but reinforced, the link. It made Bob Brand Nancy's brother-in-law. (Phyllis Brand used to call the group 'Tabloids'.) Geoffrey Dawson's wife, Cecilia, got on well with Nancy, and so did Ned Grigg's wife, Joan, who was the daughter of her old friend Anne Islington. Lionel Curtis's marriage to Pat Scott was the result of active promotion by Nancy – though as a rule she was not at all keen to see her friends marry. When a young friend, Frank Pakenham – now Lord Longford – was married in 1931 to Elizabeth Harman, Nancy said to him at the reception, in her usual bantering way: 'It's only her body you want!'

Lionel Curtis, though a remarkable and at times very compelling man, could also be the one serious bore in the group. He was nicknamed 'the Prophet', and Michael Astor has well described his awful loquacity:

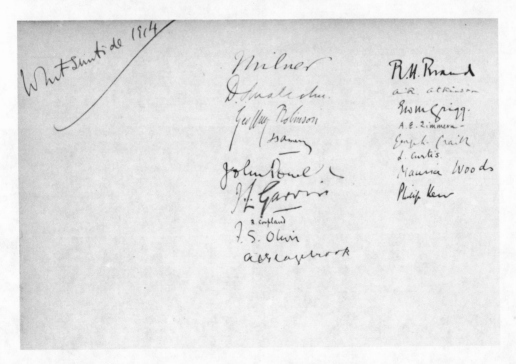

Round Table group signatures, headed by Lord Milner's, in the Cliveden visitors' book shortly before the outbreak of the First World War

Lionel Curtis on a Federated Europe evoked a sense of timelessness, of something inexorable which had to be stated and had to be heard, impervious to Bobbie's [Bobbie Shaw's] aside, voicing our unspoken thoughts, of 'Can't anyone tell him to shut up?' which carried to his end of the table and roused my mother to ask Bobbie to shut up, and through the various requests of 'shut up' Lionel boomed on, noble and unbowed.

Garvin was another great talker, who 'would go ten minutes without eating when he was talking, otherwise he lost his place'. But Garvin was less predictable than Curtis.

In 1930 Philip Kerr inherited the marquisate of Lothian and accompanying large estates. Blickling, his beautiful house in Norfolk, then became an alternative centre for the 'Tabloids'. But it did not replace Cliveden, though he himself went there rather less after acquiring a 'Camelot' of his own.

As well as the Round Table group, there were numerous other regular guests

Philip Kerr, Lord Lothian, driving from the first tee to open the Newbattle golf course, March 1935. Newbattle was one of the estates he inherited

OPPOSITE ABOVE *Bob Brand and Waldorf, on the doorstep of 3 Elliot Terrace, Plymouth, in 1923*

BELOW *Nancy, Ned Grigg and Waldorf, with three caddies, at Sandwich in 1922*

at Cliveden, who could be said to have formed part of Nancy's extended family. One of these was the equivocal Dr Thomas Jones, who was no more single-minded in his loyalty to the Astors than to the various prime ministers to whom, in turn, he acted as an *éminence grise*. Of him Michael Astor has this to say: 'He had about him a little of the wizard, whose wizardry was Welsh, persuasive and devious. His posture, both political and social, was humble and belied, in my opinion, a certain inner arrogance.'

The more traditional socio-political establishment was well represented, too. Nancy had a soft spot for Cecils and Cavendishes, and these two families were much in evidence at Cliveden. One Cavendish in-law who went there a lot in the 1930s was Harold Macmillan, and he has written of the 'two sides' of Nancy's character. She was 'deeply religious', 'the most loyal of friends' and 'ardent to support any cause which she thought might benefit humanity'. On the other hand 'she was a great hostess ... perhaps too indiscriminate in her invitations', pursuing, 'perhaps too fervently, the notabilities of the day'.

Was Nancy an indiscriminate lion-hunter? It has to be remembered that she was far from being a rich nobody whose wealth alone attracted the great. She was herself a world-famous personality, whom others in the same league – and lesser leagues – naturally wished to meet and know. Beyond question she was a royal snob: it always excited her to entertain royal personages, however tedious. But on the whole she was more interested in the contents of a bottle, as it were, than in the label (though the metaphor is perhaps rather unsuitable in her case).

As she writes in her memoir:

The strength of England is that they have no real aristocracy. Anyone's blood can become blue, for a lump sum down. . . . There is no harm in that. It is a mark of achievement. Even if the achievement is merely to have amassed a lot of money. But hereditary peerages are all wrong. . . . You might as well have a hereditary cricket team. In society there was a good deal of snobbery, and jockeying for position, but it was all very harmless and inoffensive – and there was always a leavening of people who, like myself, chose their friends because they liked them and had tastes in common, rather than for their position or wealth or because they might be useful.

In truth she was not entirely free from ordinary social snobbery. Nobody who was a royal snob could be indifferent to the charm of lineage for its own sake, and a glance at the Cliveden visitors' books suggests that some people (though not all that many) were invited for no other reason than that they had ancient and resonant names. Moreover, Nancy liked to make fun of traditions, but had no desire to destroy them. Her son Jakie says: 'She was quite conventional in a certain way. She liked to do conventional things and then turn them upside down when she was doing them. She wasn't an "outside" person.' Essentially, however, she looked for real rather than artificial quality, and her snobbery – if it can be described as such – was mainly concerned with talent and true worth. The lions that she preferred to hunt were not paper ones, and anyway she belonged to the same species herself.

Before the Great War, and before she became a great celebrity, she began to cultivate the acquaintance and friendship of eminent writers. In those days she was still reading a lot, but even when Christian Science deprived her of the habit of reading she retained an eloquence and instinctive 'feel' for words that helped to make her as fascinating to authors as they were to her. Among early literary visitors to Cliveden were Rudyard Kipling and Henry James, though neither became a 'regular'. James was taken to Cliveden by Edith Wharton in the summer of 1912, and wrote of Nancy at the time that she was 'full of possibilities and fine material – though but a reclaimed barbarian, with all her bounty, spontaneity and charm, too'.

Nancy's first writer *friend* was Hilaire Belloc, and he was a surprising one, in

Hilaire Belloc in about 1910

view of his French origin and intense Roman Catholicism. Christopher Sykes suggests that he had a bad influence on her, in that he may have aggravated the anti-Semitic prejudice that came to her from her WASP background. Their friendship was interrupted for a long time when, in 1918, Nancy tried to convert Belloc's daughters to Christian Science.

In the 1920s she got to know the legendary, perverse loner, T.E. Lawrence ('Lawrence of Arabia'), when he was serving as an aircraftman in the RAF under the name of T.E. Shaw. She was drawn to him for much the same reason, no doubt, that he was drawn to her. Both were romantic figures who could enjoy a close relationship without any unwanted demands being made on either side. For a time he was stationed at Cattewater near Plymouth, whence he wrote: 'Sandwich & Cliveden are beyond reach. So is Philip Kerr, who lives mostly in heaven, I think. Alas: selfish of him. He should join the RAF'. But Lawrence did go to Cliveden on a number of occasions, and both there and at Plymouth he scared Waldorf by taking Nancy for rides on his motor-bicycle (which was later the cause of his own death).

In one or two letters he turns to Nancy as a mother-confessor. For instance:

Everything bodily is hateful to me. . . . This sort of thing must be madness, and sometimes I wonder how far mad I am, and if a mad-house would not be my next (and merciful) stage . . . A nice neurotic letter! What you've done to deserve its receipt God knows, . . . perhaps you have listened to me too friendly-like at earlier times. . . . You are a kind of safety-valve perhaps. I wish you were an alienist.

Such self-pity is tiresome, but preferable, surely, to this: 'What a mess people make of their public, as apart from their private, affairs. If man to man ran as ill, we should all perish. Fortunately the bigger the business the less it matters.' This fatuous, pseudo-profound sentiment was uttered in 1932, on the eve of events in Europe whose manifest bigness did not, alas, make them insignificant.

But Lawrence could be delightfully clever and funny as well as bogus, and here is a letter to Nancy in which he shows to advantage:

Dear Peeress,

Three things, my memory says, upon which to congratulate you: order of merit:

(i) Personal. Your tact in ceding at golf to the Prince of Wales. That is admirable, wholly admirable. [Nancy had lost to the Prince of Wales in the semi-final of the 1933 Parliamentary golf handicap at Walton Heath, after being two up at the turn.]

(ii) Social. Your good fortune in having the new National Sporting Club as your neighbour in St James's Square. When an evening falls dull you can just step in and see a little boxing.

(iii) Dynastic. The engagement of Wissie [Nancy's daughter] as the future Lady Ancaster. Not an easy peeress to succeed, let me say. Enough said. But other aspects of it

With the Prince of Wales in the Parliamentary Golf Tournament semi-final, 1933

appeal: the financial economy, the sense of finality in marriage (not quite what it once was, perhaps, but still . . . enough said), the simplifying of your breakfast table (supposing she *did* come down to breakfast). . . . in fact the all-in-allness and honest-to-goodnessness of it. Excellent.

My own affairs march well. But it should have been Epstein and not Strobl.*

Yours proletariately
T.E. Shaw

* I refer to your affairs again, of course. Unselfish. T.E.S.

[Nancy had been sitting for a bust to the Hungarian sculptor, Kisfalud de Strobl.]

Tailpiece

The Prophet's [Lionel Curtis's] house was reduced lately to a cinder. I sent condolences and the monster replied: 'Yes, all my clothes were lost, but are well covered by insurance' . . . what would *you* put for price on the Ps clothes? . . . 'I was lucky to be sleeping at All Souls, so Pat (his wife, only) was alone in the house'.

Like another well-known hostess of the period, Lady Londonderry, Nancy was battened on by the Irish Communist playwright, Sean O'Casey, who stayed at St James's Square throughout the time that one of his plays, *Within the Gates*, was being rehearsed. But Nancy was fond of O'Casey, and when she liked somebody there was no limit to her indulgence. Her best friend among writers was, however, another Irish playwright, and a far greater one – George Bernard Shaw.

When he first met Nancy, GBS must have felt that Nature was imitating Art, or that some of his own female creations had been unconscious portraits of the real woman now before him. He and his wife, Charlotte, were both charmed by Nancy, and the friendship that developed was warmly understanding on both sides. GBS also had a sincere regard for Waldorf, whose interest in social engineering appealed to the old Fabian and vestryman of St Pancras.

As for Nancy, she was able to offer GBS, as she offered Lawrence, intimacy without any physical complications. They were alike in being clowns with a deep inner seriousness, but although they had much the same brand of humour they differed on many counts at the serious level. Consequently they made each other laugh, but did not influence each other much.

GBS agreed to have his beard trimmed and washed by Nancy's hairdresser, but did not cut his political opinions to suit hers. She, in turn, treated him as a sage without conforming to his political philosophy or – probably – reading many of his works. When a collected edition of them appeared in 1930 she asked him to send her a set, and he replied: 'Harpy, where do you think I can get a set for you? You would have to sell Cliveden to buy one. However, I'll give you mine.' But by that time she was incapable of concentrated reading, and it is unlikely that she did more than turn the pages.

[117]

Nancy with George Bernard Shaw, Cliveden, 1926

Welcoming Oxford Rhodes Scholars to Cliveden

Her company stimulated him, however, and she deserves a small share of the credit for his last great play. For it was while staying at Cliveden over Christmas in 1928 that he wrote a considerable part of *The Apple Cart*. He also read it to his fellow-guests and annoyed some of them by laughing more heartily than anybody else at his own jokes.

The atmosphere of Cliveden in Nancy's heyday can never be fully conveyed in words, but Walter Elliott, who went there as a young Conservative MP, has written of it evocatively. Nancy's way of entertaining had its origin, he says,

in the actual physical warmth, the all-embracing heat and the hospitality of the South, which was the atmosphere of her own youth. Cliveden was never more itself than in the dusk, on the high-paved terrace outside the drawing-room windows. But one always looked for the fireflies, and listened for the grasshoppers – and the mosquitoes. This was the transposition of an old theme into a new key. It added, by that much, piquancy to the whole.

And William Douglas Home, who was often at Cliveden in his youth, remembers one evening there in the 1930s when he came down to dinner early and Nancy was sitting in a chair by the fireplace reading the Bible. She did not look up when he appeared, but a moment later Sir Thomas Inskip (a well-built Conservative Cabinet minister) came in. He tripped over the light flex and she said, 'Lift up your feet, you great hulk', and went on reading the Bible. Not the way a back-bencher normally speaks to a leader of his or her party, least of all when the leader is a guest. But Nancy was no ordinary back-bencher and no ordinary hostess. That was her way with people, whoever they might be. It was her Parliamentary manner and her home manner, for both were one and the same.

7

Affectionate Bully

ℰℬ

AS a blood relation Nancy gave a lot of blood and drew a lot of blood. Whether she gave more than she drew is an open question. Her children were in the front line, and none of them escaped unscathed. At least three were major casualties. Wounds were also inflicted among the supporting troops, but even the victims would have agreed that the 'war' was a creative as well as a destructive experience.

Nancy and Waldorf were, in their different ways, tough parents. And their ways became rather less different when, after ten years, Waldorf joined Nancy in the faith of Christ Scientist. Bob Brand remarks, with the gentle irony characteristic of him, that Waldorf's conversion 'made his domestic life much easier and happier'. So it may have done, but it did not make life easier or happier for his children. As the good German that he was, he set about planning their lives and expected them to develop according to plan. Christian Science strengthened and systematized the puritanical dogmatism to which he was anyway prone. His attitude towards children and their upbringing was not unlike the Prince Consort's, with the important difference that Waldorf's intellectual demands were less rigorous (because, fortunately, he was not an intellectual) and his disciplinary methods far more humane.

By nature he was obstinate and persistent, though not overtly dominating. Nancy was the other way round. She went through life firing from the hip, and Christian Science became part of her ammunition. Though temperamentally more flexible than Waldorf, she was more assertive and therefore seemed more masterful. She was also intensely possessive – of children, other relations or friends. She could never let people who were attached to her go. They were *hers*, and her rights of ownership had to be maintained. So far as her children were concerned, the harmful effects of this possessiveness were aggravated by a good deal of neglect. Nancy was too busy to see very much of them, but when she did see them she tended to be overpowering.

Closest to her of all was her firstborn, Bobbie Shaw. In one of her pre-war

At the Oxford Drag Horse Show, in the early 1930s

The family on a visit to Mirador, September 1926

letters to Phyllis, she writes: 'Oh Phyl if I die keep Bobbie from them [his father's family]. It's my last wish & testament – don't bother about the new baby but look after Bobbie.' The 'new baby' was Bill, and the invidious relationship between him and Bobbie had tragic consequences for them both.

Bobbie was totally severed from the Shaws. After his parents' divorce he had only one brief, unsatisfactory encounter with his father, long afterwards in a London hotel. It was therefore essential for him to be properly integrated into the Astor family. This, alas, he never was. Waldorf assumed full parental responsibility for him and treated him with genuine affection; at times, too, with almost heroic forbearance. But he did not, and legally could not, give Bobbie in all respects the status of *his own* firstborn. As a result, Bill had the misfortune to come into the world as, inevitably, a rival to his mother's first and favourite child.

It would have been possible for Bobbie to take the name of Astor, but he could not be made the heir to Waldorf's peerage or the heir to Cliveden. That was Bill's destiny, and there is little doubt that his mother grudged it him. Moreover, she held it against him that he was less well favoured in looks than Bobbie or than his Astor brothers. Though ostensibly one of the most privileged children in the world, he was therefore, in a sense, cruelly disadvantaged and deprived.

The same, *mutatis mutandis*, was true of Bobbie. Though he was gifted with striking good looks, extraordinary courage and his mother's quickness of wit, he also had congenital tendencies which his upbringing did not help him to overcome. Despite being raised amid material luxury that few children could have even dreamed of, he nevertheless lacked the spiritual comfort of a home in which he could feel equal and secure. He was always conscious of being the odd man out, and not everything was done that could have been to make him feel truly a member of the Astor family. Indeed, some things were done that could only have the opposite effect.

For instance, whereas the Astor boys were all sent to Eton – Waldorf's conventional wish being that they should follow in his footsteps – Bobbie was sent to Shrewsbury, apparently because Nancy had doubts about the moral climate at Eton and in Bobbie's case she had the last word. There is no reason to suppose that, as a school, Shrewsbury was any better or any worse than Eton; certainly no

With Bobbie at Rest Harrow, Sandwich

[123]

reason to suppose that there was any difference in the moral climate, which was bound to be much of a muchness at any boys' boarding school. But it was clearly desirable that all Nancy's sons should go to the same school, or at any rate that Bobbie should not be alone in going to one school, while the others all went to another.

Later, there was a similar invidious distinction in regard to money. When Waldorf quarrelled with his father about taking a peerage, the old man changed his will and left some of the money that he would have left to Waldorf, to Waldorf's sons instead, in equal shares. Much had already been made over, and by no means the whole of the remaining estate was affected, so Waldorf did not suffer unduly. But his sons benefited to the extent of becoming millionaires as soon as they were twenty-one. Bobbie had no such independence. Though there was plenty of Shaw money earmarked for his benefit, Nancy had the control of it and never surrendered that control. Whereas the Astor boys were financially (if not psychologically) free from the moment they came of age, Bobbie was kept on a string by his mother until she was dead and he an elderly man. In practice, he was seldom as badly off as he used to make out. Complaining about poverty was an expression partly of his general resentments and partly of a rather obsessive meanness in money matters. But it *was* true that he remained ultimately dependent for funds upon Nancy, and that in this he differed from his half-brothers.

No doubt he was born with a strong homosexual tendency, but whether or not it was inevitable that he should become a confirmed homosexual will never be known. Clearly the circumstances of his life were unhelpful, as any amateur psychologist can see. Was his mother aware of the tendency? According to one view, she did not know of the existence of homosexuality, but this is hard to believe. There are, surely, different levels of knowledge. Some things are known and freely discussed; others known and not discussed; others known, as it were, *in pectore* but not admitted even to oneself. Nancy lived at a time when much that was known was not talked about. (Today everything is talked about without necessarily being very well understood.) If Nancy decided against sending Bobbie to Eton because she had heard ugly rumours, the rumours cannot have been meaningless to her. Probably she knew about homosexuality but did not discuss it; probably, too, she sensed that Bobbie was homosexual but was reluctant to admit it, even to herself. However that may be, he soon became involved in homosexual situations. When he was a child in the Highlands a priest gave him a ring, which Nancy found him wearing. He may have been seduced at an early age by Lord Kitchener, whose country home, Broome Park, was within easy reach of Rest Harrow. Bobbie used to say that Kitchener's famous poster had, for him, a personal rather than patriotic significance.

[124]

With Bill at Henley

As an officer in the Blues he was able to practise the horsemanship at which he excelled. He won many races, including the Royal Military Gold Cup, but he also had a terrible accident that nearly cost him his life. Such was his courage that he was soon racing again, but to protect his injured head he devised the cork-lined jockey's cap that has since become standard wear.

Peace-time soldiering held even worse dangers for him than falls on the race-course. One of his weaknesses was drink, and eventually he was thrown out of the Blues for being drunk on duty. Soon afterwards, in 1931, he was caught committing a homosexual offence, tried, convicted and sent to prison. He could have avoided arrest by going abroad, but preferred to stay in England and face the consequences. (Elizabeth Langhorne – a relation by marriage, and a biographer of Nancy – suggests that his decision to go to gaol may also have been 'part of the savage, half-unconscious war waged by Bobbie and his mother'. But unwillingness to become an exile was a sufficient motive.)

The scandal was hushed up. Waldorf was a newspaper proprietor and other propietors showed 'trade union' solidarity. At Cliveden Mr Lee assembled all the servants, gave them a vague indication of the family crisis, and then said: 'After you leave the servants' hall no one will speak about the matter. Anyone heard or suspected of doing so in or out of the house will be instantly dismissed.' All the same, Bobbie was a broken man.

Nancy and Waldorf stood by him, of course, and on the surface his position, when he emerged from the Scrubs, was unchanged. But in reality what had happened made his dependence upon Nancy more abject and painful than ever. No two people knew better how to hurt each other, and they did so increasingly. Bobbie was a familiar, mocking presence in the Astors' Camelot, combining the functions of a Shakespearean fool and a Shakespearean bastard. He could be lovable or he could be brutal, but either way his wit was paramount.

If Bobbie suffered from an excess of (unwise and misapplied) mother-love, Bill suffered no less acutely from the lack of it. He deserved better. Unlike his father he got a respectable degree at Oxford, in spite of being ill during his last year. He had distinct ability. Above all, he had his father's conscientiousness and the kind-heartedness of both his parents. But sadly he had less than his fair share of the family charm, and none of Nancy's brash self-confidence.

He was elected to Parliament in 1935, but as a new MP had his mother as much on top of him there as she was at home. Before long his political career was interrupted by the Second World War, and then by defeat at the 1945 general election. After returning to the House of Commons in 1951 he soon had to leave it again, when his father died. Until near the end of his life he was unable to create any domestic stability for himself. He married comparatively late, and his first two marriages came to grief swiftly. In retrospect, there seems to have been a curse on

[126]

OPPOSITE ABOVE *Silver wedding day, 3 May 1931: left to right, Bobbie, Wissie, Michael, Bill, Nancy, Waldorf, Jakie, David*

BELOW *Eight years later: left to right, Bill, Bobbie, Wissie, Nancy, David, Michael, Jakie*

his life, and to some extent it was, unquestionably, a maternal curse.

The other outstanding victim among the Astor children was the daughter. Difficult as it was to be one of Nancy's sons, it was perhaps even more difficult to be her only daughter. Nancy once told Michael that she would have liked him to be a *plain daughter* – a joke, of course, but with just a grain of underlying truth. Wissie was by no means plain, so she could not help being, in a sense, a challenge to Nancy, without meaning to be. Nancy tried to dominate her; she fought against the attempted domination; and the fight left its emotional scars.

More serious, however, was a physical consequence of the relationship. In 1929 Wissie had a hunting accident, in which her spine was badly injured. She was staying with her cousin Nancy Tree (now Nancy Lancaster) who saw to it that Wissie was brought back to her house from the scene of the accident, attended by a doctor. Before long, Nancy and Waldorf arrived with a Christian Science practitioner and – surprisingly – a radiographer. The sequel has been variously described, and the versions seem to be contradictory; but there is no doubt at all that Wissie's back plagued her for the rest of her life and that she herself felt that it had not been properly treated at the time. According to Nancy Lancaster, there was no veto by Wissie's parents on orthodox medical treatment for her back, but instead she was urged to choose between such treatment and Christian Science. Granted the background of indoctrination, this was hardly a fair choice. In all probability she tried to cure herself by Christian Science, but without success, and in doing so forfeited whatever chance she might have had of being cured by more orthodox means. In 1933 she married Lord Willoughby de Eresby (now Lord Ancaster) and so became relatively independent of Nancy. But she never ceased to bear the marks of her earlier subjugation.

The other three children – David, Michael and Jakie – were in varying degrees affected by their mother's personality, though less harmfully than the three eldest. David was for a time cherished by Nancy as Bill never was, but conflict began when his political views developed on mildly left-wing lines. Later, he grew very close to Waldorf at a time when Nancy and Waldorf were (as will be seen) estranged. She disapproved of much that the *Observer* stood for in the 1950s, under David's very successful editorship. But for all her disapproval she was also rather proud of his success. Moreover she entirely shared his feeling for the underdog, however much she might deplore the political opinions into which it led him.

Michael, who was perhaps her favourite Astor son, was the least Astor-ish of them and came nearest to detaching himself from his parents' magnetic field. By nature an aesthete, he did not feel drawn to the military career that his father had in mind for him, though he served in the army during the war. His rebellion was in the direction of becoming a dilettante in the good sense, as painter, author and patron of the arts. For a short time after the war he was an MP, but soon found that

Parliament did not suit him at all. His book *Tribal Feeling*, published while Nancy was still alive, shows his quality as a writer and the extent of his detachment. In one of many remarkable passages he helps us to understand the disturbing character of the family life that he experienced:

Despite enchanting moments when the family felt happily united, moments that were infinitely reassuring, it was usually a relief when there were outsiders present. When we were just the family all sense of personal privacy evaporated. Visitors, especially if they were what I thought of as 'worldly' rather than 'religious' people, formed a silent court of appeal, their presence imposing a modicum of restraint.

The paradox that there could be no privacy when the family was on its own is surely most striking.

Jakie seems to have been the least troubled of the children. It may have been an advantage to be the youngest and in any case his temperament is the most extrovert. Without any of Bobbie's problems, he was like Bobbie in being able to repay Nancy in her own coin, having the same quick wit and disconcerting directness. At the same time he has Waldorf's passion for order and organization. Even he, however, bears some traces of the conflict and stress that Michael describes, and when in 1944 he married a Roman Catholic Argentinian, Ana Inez

Nancy Tree, later Lancaster

[129]

(Chiquita) Cárcano, neither of his parents would attend the wedding. After this, he admits, he 'never felt quite the same' about Nancy, though his affection for her remained very strong.

Every morning the children would be given a Christian Science lesson by their parents, which Bobbie did not attend. David believes that he was rather hurt at being excluded, and recalls how he made fun of the lessons as an outsider. Having tried to join the class one day, and having been shooed away by Nancy, he sat outside the room reading a paper. When the others emerged he struck an attitude of prayer and said with unction: 'I knew, I knew – when I heard a noise like a bull-fight it must be the Bible class.'

Despite all the puritanical indoctrination, Nancy's humour was always breaking through, and there were also hints of a worldly wisdom far removed from the dictates of Mrs Baker Eddy. Michael once told the writer of a curious incident when he was about nineteen, which puzzled him to the end of his life. He arrived at Cliveden one weekend with a 'blonde and beautiful' model, feeling 'like a kind of Clumber spaniel with a huge pheasant in its mouth'. The girl came down to dinner rather too *décolletée*, he thought, for prudence, and at the same time it suddenly struck him that the colour of her hair was not natural. But the real surprise was that his mother had given her the bedroom next to his own. 'I never knew whether this was because she thought it didn't matter, or whether she accepted the fact that Michael was having an affair with a blonde model', and might as well get it out of his system. If the second interpretation is correct, she was acting more as a realistic Edwardian than as an idealistic Eddyite.

As well as the children of the house, there were usually other relations at Cliveden. With the exception of Lizzie, Nancy's sisters were often there, particularly Phyllis and Nora. Lizzie, the eldest sister, had spanked Nancy as a child more than their mother did, but Nancy was able to get her own back later. She sent Lizzie, who was hard up, a regular allowance, but insisted that she account for the spending of every dollar of it. After Lizzie's death she regretted this churlish behaviour and tried to atone for it by lavishing affection on Lizzie's children.

Nancy, the elder daughter, was first married to a Marshall Field, who died very soon leaving her immensely rich. She then married another rich man, Ronald Tree, so she was able to deal with her aunt on terms of financial equality. Alice, the younger daughter, was probably the closer of the two to Nancy (Astor) until the last phase of her life. She is married to Reginald Winn and lived for a time at Taplow Lodge within the Astors' orbit. Her children Elizabeth and Anne, and later David, were very much part of the Cliveden scene.

Irene and Dana Gibson came there fairly often, but their home was in America. Phyllis remained Nancy's favourite sister, and after marrying Bob Brand

[130]

Phyllis Brand

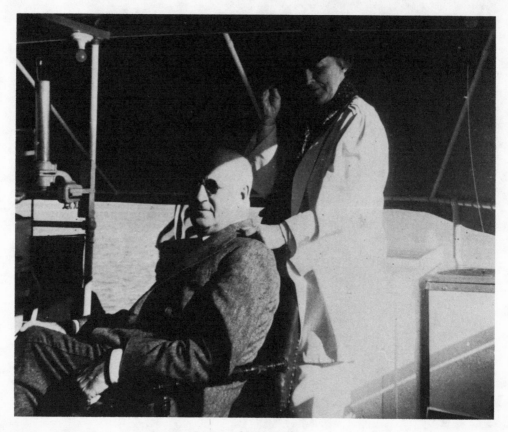

Irene and Dana Gibson

she lived in England. When she died of pneumonia in 1937, Nancy broke down as she very seldom did; Rose Harrison found her 'screaming, crying and praying'. Phyllis's children – Virginia, Dinah and Jim – thereafter meant more than ever to her, and when Jim was killed at the very end of the war it was as if she had lost one of her own sons.

Nora, Nancy's youngest sister, was a huge success with men, and they with her. To use a somewhat dated word, she was flighty. But she was also great fun, and her gifts as a comedian and musician helped to make any party go. With her husband, Paul Phipps – whom she later abandoned – she, too, lived for a time on the Cliveden estate, and her two children, Tommy and Joyce, were welcome, if rather poor, relations at the big house.

Joyce then showed little of the wholesome glamour and disciplined talent that made her, as Joyce Grenfell, a household name. She never forgot the effect that her Aunt Nancy had upon a shy, ungainly child. 'I was scared to death of her.

Silhouette of Nancy, with Joyce Grenfell and Alice Winn, Cliveden

She was a great tease and I was extremely mockable, because I was fat and had no sense of humour and took myself very seriously and cried at the drop of a hat.' Nancy made many of her relations cry, young and old, though she seldom cried herself. One of Joyce Grenfell's less pleasant memories was of arriving late for a meal at Cliveden, when there was a large house party and, say, twenty people were already sitting at the table in the dining-room. Nancy was a stickler for punctuality in others, though extremely unpunctual herself.

I was late for lunch, I remember, and it was a daunting arrival. I had to slip in, or try to slip in, but she said: 'Where have you been and what do you think you're doin'?' It was a form of bullying. I now know it had some affection in it, because she was an affectionate bully. But I'm not sure I felt so at the time.

It would be easy to say that Nancy had a generous heart but no sensitiveness. Yet this would be to oversimplify her complex character. Certainly she *could* be insensitive – as when, for instance, talking to an old friend, Elsie Lansdowne, late in the Second World War, she complained at length about the anxiety of having four sons in the armed forces, oblivious of the fact that Elsie had lost all three of her sons, two of them killed in action. In such cases, Nancy was simply talking without thinking.

But if her mind was not abstracted or absorbed in her own problems, she could have an almost uncanny insight into another person's thoughts and feelings. She was capable of true sympathy – when she was in a sympathetic mood. Even when she was in a bullying mood she was not necessarily insensitive. Her faculty of insight would then, unfortunately, become a power of darkness, because it enabled her to sense another person's weak spots, which she would be likely to attack for all she was worth. Having a thick skin herself, she expected others to be able to take, even to enjoy, her rough treatment. But not everybody could take it, and not everybody who suffered from it won through, as Joyce Grenfell did, to an appreciation of the love and generosity that the bullying disguised. For Nancy it was a sort of game; for most others, a torment.

People of all ages, but more especially children, were apt to be bewildered by her; and her own children, who bore the chief brunt of her alternating moods, were of course the most bewildered of all. Two qualities most desirable in a parent she did not possess – calm and the readiness to praise. Partly because she was trying to do so much, but also because of her own temperament, she conveyed a sense of perpetual restlessness. Her eyes were those of a colt not yet broken in, 'tameless and swift and proud'. They flashed humour, joy, exhilaration, love; or annoyance, impatience, aggression, mockery. They did not convey peace.

Her inability to praise is noted by Rose Harrison. 'She was unpredictable and always unappreciative'. And one head gardener at Cliveden, Frank Copcutt, said that 'her ladyship was not much given to paying compliments'. She rewarded people in other ways – by amusing them, by treating them as equals, by innumerable acts of kindness. But she could not give the immediate word of encouragement or reassurance that a child, in particular, so badly needs.

When faced with mutiny, her last line of defence – or attack – was always her sense of fun. This was what Rose most loved about her, and others who had to struggle with her at close quarters would have agreed. When Mr Lee once said, in exasperation, that he was leaving, Nancy asked him to let her know where he was going so that she could come too. On one occasion David, as a young man, was determined not to stay an extra night at Cliveden (though he had no pressing reason to be elsewhere) because his mother was making an issue of it. The argument was angry and protracted, but at last, seeing that she could not get her own way, she suddenly changed tone. 'If you happen to see your mother,' she said, 'do give her my regards. They tell me she's a really nice woman.'

In a sense the mythical 'they' were right. Nancy was really good. But it has to be said that the adverb covered a few flaws and perversities.

8

Apostle of Detente

꧁ꕥ꧂

N ANCY'S record in foreign affairs has earned her much misunderstanding. For a time it was thought to be not only bad but sinister. In fact her
views on foreign policy, though in many ways naïve and superficial, were
also consistent and very largely honourable. Since the subject was one on which
she had little first-hand knowledge, she tended to rely too much upon the opinions
of others. As a result she made one huge, disastrous error, but she made it openly
and in good company. (Of this, later in the chapter.)

She had no belief at all in Continental alliances, but she did believe – it was
her deepest conviction – that the English-speaking nations had a mission to work
together for the good of humanity. In this she anticipated the dream that was later
to bemuse Winston Churchill, with whom she so often disagreed on other matters.
In 1922 she spoke in New York words that might have been quoted from Churchill
twenty years on:

I do say that if the greatest commonwealth of nations the world has ever seen and the
greatest federation of states the world has ever known cannot be brought together by some
common cause, some human hope and purpose, then . . . the spirit would go out of me. I do
believe that these two nations are bound together by a common cause; and that cause . . .
is peace on earth and goodwill toward all men.

Such words are very splendid, but they gloss over awkward facts of geography and
irreducible conflicts of interest. Like Churchill later, Nancy felt that she was herself
a symbol and embodiment of the Anglo-American unity that could be made
effective at the political level. She saw no reason why her own marriage should not
serve as an example of political marriage to her 'two nations'. Greeted with
rapture in America after her election to Parliament, she naturally fell into the trap
of overrating her influence with her former compatriots.

All the same, it was not wrong to do all that she could to improve Anglo-
American relations, and she never tired in her efforts. American ambassadors and
their families were entertained by her as a matter of course, and were thus

With Felix Frankfurter at Oxford, 1939

introduced to a wider circle than they would otherwise have known, since before the Second World War American ambassadors did not count for much, socially. The young Kennedys were no strangers to Cliveden, when their father was ambassador in London. (So there was, after all, some link between the two 'Camelots'.) The list of famous Americans who stayed at Cliveden is impressive. On one page of the visitors' book for 1918 there is the signature of Franklin D. Roosevelt, who was then Assistant Secretary of the Navy in the Woodrow Wilson administration. (His name appears not far below those of David and Margaret Lloyd George, who made Cliveden an exception to their rule of not staying in English stately homes.) Two others who stayed were Henry Ford and his wife, he signing his name 'Henry Ford', she signing hers – rather quaintly – 'Mrs Henry Ford'.

But Nancy's hospitality was never confined to VIPs. Unknown, as well as known, Americans went to Cliveden in droves. One who was prevented, by bad luck, from spending a weekend there was Verne A. Ferguson, now president of the Danville Historical Society, whose experience provides a vivid glimpse of Nancy in

On the terrace at Cliveden with (left to right) Henry Ford, Mrs Henry Ford and Bill, 1926

[139]

OPPOSITE *With Franklin D. Roosevelt at Hyde Park, autumn 1932*

action. Mr Ferguson was a child in Danville when Nancy paid a triumphal visit to her birthplace not long after being elected to Parliament. She visited his school and presented each child in the first grade with a rose-bush, to mark the occasion. During the Second World War, before his country was involved, Mr Ferguson volunteered for service in the Royal Canadian Air Force, and in due course was posted to England. One day he went to the House of Commons, because he wanted to thank Nancy again for her present. He sent in a ticket and she came out to see him. Very soon afterwards he was posted to West Africa, where some time later he received a letter from her, forwarded from England, inviting him to spend a weekend at Cliveden. By then the weekend was long past – but his gratitude remains.

While clinging to the idea of Anglo-American solidarity as the key to salvation for the world, Nancy at the same time stood for a policy of peace with all nations, however unregenerate their peoples or unsavoury their rulers. In this spirit she made, in the summer of 1931, a highly publicized trip to the Soviet Union, which was a most surprising and daring thing for a Conservative politician, at that date, to do. She went with Waldorf, David, Philip Lothian and, above all, Bernard Shaw, who was the one whom the Russians had actually asked, but who insisted (David thinks as a practical joke) that he should be allowed to bring his plutocratic friends with him. Just before they were due to leave Bobbie Shaw's case blew up, but the Astors decided that to cancel the journey would only arouse curiosity as to why they were not going.

The party travelled across Europe by train, and then spent ten days in the Soviet Union. While they were in Moscow, GBS, Nancy, Waldorf and Lothian had an interview with Stalin, at which Nancy had the nerve to ask him why he was slaughtering so many Russians. The interpreters were afraid to translate the question, but Stalin ordered them to do so, and then replied that many people had to die before the Communist State could be firmly established.

Earlier, she had made a speech defending capitalism to a crowd of workers in a Moscow factory. And when taken by her Intourist guide to a jewellery shop, she said: 'I never buy stolen goods.' But GBS was the guest of honour, and wherever they went he praised the Soviet system to the skies. He continued to do so after their return home, when he spoke to the Press and, at length, to the ILP summer school. Lothian was invited to give *his* impressions to the Liberal summer school, but Nancy received no request to address any similar audience of Conservatives.

Instead she gave an account of her trip to the *Christian Science Monitor*, and her comments read as more balanced and realistic than either GBS's on the one hand or those of the average Western anti-Bolshie on the other. There is no doubt, she says, about the tyranny that is ushering in the new dispensation in Russia. 'The ruling caste is making a deliberate attempt to burn into the national

[141]

Lloyd George at Cliveden, 1921. L'après-midi d'un faune?

consciousness dogmas which obliterate the individual personality and many of the things that we in the West hold most dear.' Yet the new Russia must be seen in perspective. 'It's no use simply applying the standards of the more or less comfortable classes in the home country. . . . Russian society must be judged not according to modern standards at all but according to medieval conceptions.' Gradually the regime might evolve towards mercy and justice. Meanwhile, she concludes, 'Trade with Russia, treat it like any other country, but don't try to interfere with its way of doing things. I am certain that is our best way of helping to light some of the dark spots.'

Her philosophy, clearly, was that which has come to be known as détente, or peaceful co-existence. Applied to the Soviet Union it was, and within reason still is, a sensible policy. But Nancy came under heavy attack from Winston Churchill, who denounced her indiscriminately, along with GBS, in a newspaper article later included in *Great Contemporaries*:

The Russians have always been fond of travelling-shows and circuses, and here was the world's most famous intellectual clown and pantaloon in one, and the charming Columbine of the capitalist pantomime. So the crowds were marshalled, thousands were served out with their red scarves and flags . . . and the Arch-Commissar, Stalin, the man of steel, throwing open the closely-guarded sanctuary of the Kremlin, and pushing aside his morning budget of death warrants and *lettres de cachet*, received his guests with smiles of unaffected comradeship.

It was unfair to bracket Nancy so closely with GBS, because their reactions to the Soviet Union were markedly different. But Churchill was never fair to Nancy, and at this time he had another reason for being annoyed with her. While he was beginning to lead a rearguard action against even the most modest constitutional reform in India, she was open-minded on the Indian question and capable of responding to a well-stated case for drastic reform.

Such a statement she received from Gandhi himself, while he was in London for the Round Table Conference in the autumn of 1931. She asked him to St James's Square and they established a considerable rapport. Both were very humorous as well as very religious, and Gandhi, as the supreme champion of women's rights in his own country, was naturally sympathetic towards Nancy. He did not mind being ragged by her. When she presumed to say that he was not a holy man at all, but just another crafty politician, he was thoroughly amused. But when she said that his policies were merely destructive, he asked her quietly if she would like to listen to him or would rather go on talking. She listened. At dinner he got his own back by ragging her. When she offered him American pecan nuts, he exclaimed in mock-horror: 'Oh Lady Astor, be British and buy British.'

Unfortunately she never went to India, and her interest in the subject never developed beyond the point of vague progressiveness and goodwill. But at least she

OPPOSITE ABOVE *With Waldorf and Bernard Shaw, Red Square, Moscow, July 1931*
BELOW *With Bernard Shaw and (centre) Maxim Litvinov, Russia, July 1931. Later Litvinov stayed at Cliveden, where he joined in the match-box game, nose to nose*

had the urge to meet Gandhi, and when she met him was to some extent influenced by him. If she could have communed with him further, he might conceivably have taught her to be less narrowly dogmatic in religion, and to draw some inspiration from faiths other than her own.

It is for her attitude to Nazi Germany that Nancy has been most adversely judged, and this was, of course, the outstanding foreign affairs issue of the 1930s. Her approach to it was the same as to the Soviet Union. She hated the Nazi tyranny as much as she hated the Bolshevik tyranny, but felt that the democracies had to live with it, since the only alternative was war. So far, so good – but her thinking did not go far enough. She failed to perceive the all-important differences between Nazi Germany and the Soviet Union, and between the personalities of the two tyrants. Whereas the Soviet Union was a backward state with vast internal problems and no need to expand territorially, Hitler's Germany was irredentist, imperialist and technologically a match for any other state in Europe. Moreover, whereas Stalin was a cautious and rational monster, Hitler was a monster who

Nancy and Waldorf with (far left) Philip Lothian, at Walter Elliot's wedding

was reckless and, despite appearances that took many people in, fundamentally mad.

Perhaps it was a pity that she never met Hitler. Waldorf had interviews with both Hitler and Mussolini, but Nancy was not with him on either occasion. At his meeting with Hitler, as part of a Christian Science delegation, he raised the Jewish question and was shaken by the violence of Hitler's reaction. It is just possible that Nancy might have realized, if she had come face to face with the Führer, that he was not a man with whom the democracies could ever negotiate a stable settlement.

As it was, she took his claims and grievances too seriously, feeling that if they could be satisfied peace would be assured. In this she was much influenced by Lothian, who had a bad conscience about the Versailles Treaty, of which he had been one of the authors (as Lloyd George's chief aide). But her judgement was also distorted by her prejudice against France, a country that she once described to Bob Brand as 'nothing but one big brothel'. Such a view of Britain's principal ally was unhelpful in the circumstances.

Another, and overlapping, prejudice was that against Roman Catholicism, which further warped her thinking on European issues. Early in 1937 she told David's German friend, the anti-Nazi Rhodes Scholar Adam von Trott, that his country was quite right to rearm seeing that it was surrounded by hostile Roman Catholic powers. The fact that she could regard France as a Roman Catholic power betrays the depth of her ignorance; but above all it was dangerous to say anything that might appear to justify Hitler's propaganda about the 'encirclement' of Germany.

All the more so, as her German contacts during this period were not confined to anti-Nazis. In 1936 Joachim von Ribbentrop paid several visits to England as Hitler's representative, before being formally appointed ambassador in the autumn. He met the Astors and was asked to lunch at St James's Square. David reluctantly attended this lunch, and still recalls the embarrassment and cross-purposes of the occasion:

My mother tried to treat [Ribbentrop] in her ordinary light way. Towards the end of the meal she said, 'Tell us a bit about your master, but I must warn you that anyone with a Charlie Chaplin moustache is never going to be taken seriously by the British public.' Ribbentrop, who had as much humour as your left foot, sat there frozen and horrified and didn't make any reply. He left the lunch fairly early and that was that. It was a magnificent failure.

But it was not Ribbentrop's only experience of the Astors' hospitality. Dame Irene Ward remembered being asked to a dinner at St James's Square, to meet him. After dinner there was a game of musical chairs and Nancy whispered to the

[145]

British guests that they should let Ribbentrop win. He was never asked to Cliveden, but there was one important meeting between him and Nancy at Sandwich.

The initiative for this came from Tom Jones, who was trying to arrange a meeting between his master, Baldwin, and Hitler. One afternoon in early June 1936 he proposed bringing Ribbentrop to Rest Harrow, where he would meet Sir Thomas Inskip, Minister for the Co-ordination of Defence (the man who was so brusquely spoken to by Nancy when he tripped over the flex at Cliveden). They arrived in time for dinner. Waldorf was away at Geneva, but Lothian was there and made up the party. According to Jones's account, Inskip – who was a fervent evangelical Churchman – questioned Ribbentrop about the Nazi persecution of Christians. Ribbentrop replied that 'a new Reformation' was occurring in Germany, and Nancy threw in a characteristic *mot*: 'The Roman Catholics make God material and the Communists make man material.' The discussion of politics was rambling and inconclusive, though it cannot have encouraged Ribbentrop to believe that Britain would tolerate any revision of the Versailles settlement by force. When Jones referred to the strength of British public support for the League of Nations, Lothian unwisely suggested that this had been undermined by the fall of Abyssinia. But Nancy endorsed what Jones had said.

Her attitude towards Germany was exactly the same in private as it was in public. She hated the regime, as she hated all tyrannies, but she wanted to preserve the peace of Europe by negotiation. And it seemed to her that there must be top-level contacts between Britain and Germany. It did not occur to her that the mere fact of talking 'out of school' to Ribbentrop could create a false impression.

When Neville Chamberlain succeeded Baldwin as Prime Minister in May 1937, and soon revealed his intention of trying to save the peace by personal diplomacy, Nancy became one of his most enthusiastic supporters. How could it have been otherwise, granted her naïve belief, which so resembled his own, that the causes of conflict could be spirited away if only the principals got together? It is worth mentioning, too, that in the 1920s Chamberlain had been the sort of social-reforming minister that the Astors most admired.

Nancy's blind support for Chamberlainite appeasement was the worst political mistake of her career. But it cannot be emphasized too strongly that the policy was *Chamberlain's*, owing nothing at all to alleged behind-the-scenes machinations by the Astors. The myth imputing blame to them was started by the gifted Communist journalist Claud Cockburn who, in his small-circulation paper *The Week*, launched the idea of a conspiratorial 'Cliveden Set' engineering a sell-out to the Nazis so that Hitler could become the tool of Western plutocrats against Bolshevism.

The 'evidence' for this conspiracy theory was either untrue or grossly misleading. For instance, one of *The Week's* first attacks was concerned with a mission to Germany by Lord Halifax, Lord President of the Council. This, it was said, had been arranged at Cliveden, behind the back of the Foreign Secretary, Anthony Eden. In fact, Eden had spent the weekend in question at Cliveden, though Halifax had not. Mr Cockburn's subsequent attempt to explain this preposterous inaccuracy away has its place among the marvels of journalistic effrontery.

All the same, the basic story was taken up by other newpapers and treated with undue respect by foreign embassies. No doubt Mr Cockburn believed it himself (he still does), and whatever his merits as an investigative journalist he is a

Group at Cliveden, including Elsie Lansdowne (far left), Geoffrey Dawson (centre) and Joan Grigg (far right)

delightfully witty man, who could keep his small but influential readership amused with reports from 'Schloss' Cliveden. During Britain's last phase as a super-power, foreigners were still easily convinced that British policy was formed by arcane, Machiavellian processes, and the Cliveden Set theory fitted neatly into the imaginary pattern.

But surely the main reason for the myth's growing – and lasting – currency is that it offered a scapegoat for the general failure to stop Hitler, and more especially for the failure of the Left to evolve any credible policy of resistance. For Socialists of all denominations it was supremely convenient to be able to ascribe all the guilt of appeasement to a small group of people meeting in the country house of a Conservative millionaire, and of his wife who was a Conservative MP. To dispirited and disunited class warriors the Cliveden Set was an answer to prayer. In this case, as in so many others, myth was more comforting than truth.

The story gained plausibility from the role of Geoffrey Dawson, editor of *The Times* (whose chief proprietor was Waldorf's brother, John). Dawson was certainly an arch-appeaser, and he was also very often at Cliveden. But the true Cliveden Set, the inner circle of Astor friends of which he was a member, was in fact sharply divided over appeasement. Dawson and Lothian were, like the Astors themselves, strongly in favour of the policy. Brand, Grigg and Hichens were no less strongly against it. (Curtis's attitude is harder to define.) Moreover, some of the Astors' close friends outside the Round Table group, such as Lord Cranborne and Harold Macmillan, were among the policy's most committed opponents.

The position of the *Observer* – the paper that Waldorf himself owned – needs to be explained. Garvin, the editor, was certainly a Cliveden figure and up to a point he stood for the policy of appeasement. But he believed in negotiation from strength and was, therefore, an impassioned advocate of rearmament. Moreover, though he defended the Munich agreement, he changed course abruptly a fortnight later, when comment in Germany convinced him that Hitler's ambitions were unlimited. He cannot, therefore, be regarded as a 'pure' appeaser.

Nancy was outraged by what she regarded as a smear campaign, and when John Strachey introduced her one day to Mr Cockburn, in the Central Lobby of the House of Commons, she did not speak to him but spat. As Chillie Langhorne's daughter, spitting perhaps came naturally to her. She was the last person in the world to engage in any conspiracy, least of all a nefarious one. Her character was open, to a fault. But in the late 1930s her non-conspiratorial activities only served to reinforce the myth, once it had caught on.

In May 1938 she gave a lunch at St James's Square to enable Chamberlain to meet American correspondents. At this lunch Chamberlain suggested that Czechoslovakia should cede the Sudetenland to Germany, a demand that Hitler himself had not yet made. No such suggestion had been put forward by Nancy or

J. L. Garvin attitudinising, 1924

Exterior of the Astors' London house, 4 St James's Square, as it is today

Waldorf, but inevitably they were involved in guilt by association. In any case they continued to follow the Prime Minister, despite the appalling remark made in their house, which foreshadowed the Munich surrender later in the year. But Nancy was surely justified in saying that if they had been hatching a pro-Nazi plot they would not have invited American journalists as witnesses.

Shortly beforehand, she had used her *entrée* at the German embassy to do a good turn to one of her American friends, the eminent Jewish lawyer, Felix Frankfurter. An uncle of his who lived in Vienna was arrested by the invading Nazis at the time of the *Anschluss*, and Frankfurter appealed to Nancy to do whatever she could to secure his release. She went at once to Ribbentrop's successor, von Dirksen, and threatened to descend on Vienna herself if the uncle were not immediately set free. He was set free.

Thanking her for her 'prompt and effective intervention', Frankfurter at the same time reproached her for supporting the appeasement policy. But having done so, he added: 'my deep disagreement with you in your estimate of the forces

Lower dining room at 4 St James's Square, with the table laid for an American Independence Day party, 1930. The Sargent portrait of Nancy has been brought up from Cliveden

now struggling for mastery in the world is wholly unrelated to my knowledge of your personal warm-heartedness and the generosity of your feelings.' In a letter to him which, though undated, seems to be an answer, Nancy gives an apologia for her position:

With regard to the 'Cliveden Set' . . . there is not one word of truth in all this propaganda. . . . It is an attempt to create suspicion and a class war [and] is now being used by the Communist, Socialist and Liberal Oppositions in their effort to bring down the Government. Unfortunately a lot of journalists have seized it as 'good copy'. As you know, Philip Lothian and Waldorf have believed for about fifteen years that something should have been done in the re-organization of Europe, so as to rectify some of the mistakes of the Peace Treaties and remedy some of Germany's grievances. It was plainly impossible to keep Germany permanently down. . . . Unfortunately by not making voluntarily certain concessions to Germany, we have made them feel that they can only get redress by force.

[151]

I loathe all Dictatorships whether of the Russian or German type. They are all equally cruel.

Some years ago I fought for a Trade Pact with Russia . . . and I was then called a Communist.

Today I have supported those who wanted to improve relations between Britain and Germany and between Britain and Italy, and now I am called a Fascist.

I am neither.

The last statement was entirely true. Indeed, while she was being attacked by the Communist *Week*, she was also being attacked by the Fascist *Action*. She had nothing whatever to do with Oswald Mosley after he turned towards extremist politics. He ceased to be invited to Cliveden and, as he himself puts it: 'She remained a very democratic person and was not at all interested in our kind of thing.'

Yet she was out of her depth in the dark and turbulent waters of the 1930s. It was not true that all dictatorships were 'equally cruel', and even if it had been true the remark would still have been irrelevant to the crucial issue, which was whether or not it was safe to make unilateral concessions to Hitler. As well as being cruel on a larger scale than any other dictator except Stalin, Hitler was more of a gambler, more unstable and more crazily obsessed than any other important tyrant in the world. He could not be treated as just another unpleasant foreigner, but had to be dealt with as a case apart. Everyone can now see that this was so. Some – but not, alas, Nancy – could see it at the time.

A few of Nancy's remarks during the appeasement period were deplorable as well as silly. It was unworthy of her, for instance, to suggest off the cuff in the House of Commons that Sudeten German refugees were Communists who should be sent to Russia. But on the whole her record is one of simple wrong-headedness, resulting far more from misapplied and undiscriminating goodwill than from any bad motives. Her delusion was shared by most British people, including King George VI and Queen Elizabeth, who appeared with Chamberlain on the balcony of Buckingham Palace after Munich.

When the appeasement policy collapsed, with Hitler's march into Prague in March 1939, Nancy the appeaser was swiftly transformed into Nancy the fighter. The transformation was natural enough; her temperament was more pugnacious than accommodating. She turned against Hitler with all the fury, not of a woman scorned, but of a born crusader out to destroy implacable evil. The Nazis were right to put her on their black list; they had no more relentless enemy in Britain.

In the political crisis that followed the Norwegian disaster in the spring of 1940, she showed more toughness than most Conservatives. At the end of the vital Commons debate on 7–8 May she was one of the forty Conservative MPs who voted with Labour against the Government. Faithful though she was to friends, at that desperate moment her loyalty to the country superseded her loyalty to Chamberlain.

Mathematically, he did not lose the vote. Most Conservatives still supported him, and he still had a majority in Parliament. But morally he was defeated, and when he found that Labour would not serve under him in a coalition government he resigned. The consequence of the action that Nancy and others had taken was that Winston Churchill became Prime Minister – though it was not a consequence that most expected or many wished. The vote had been anti-Chamberlain, but only to a limited extent pro-Churchill.

Soon, however, it was apparent that the result was providential, and Nancy should have her share of the credit for bringing the right man to power. In view of the relations between them, the situation was ironic. She always said that he was a great war leader in 1940, though he showed no gratitude to her for helping to make his apotheosis possible.

During the critical summer of 1940 she wrote to a correspondent in New York:

It seems to me that the best thing that ever came out of the East was Jesus Christ, and I am afraid it is pretty evident that until all peoples accept the Christ we shall have no peace. Remember Ghandi [*sic*] would never have known of the Christ if the British had not been in India, he would still have believed in that strange religion Hinduism.

I don't believe that the British are going to lose this war, but I do believe that America is going to find that she has got to do her bit before it is over.

I am sorry for the French, Democracy isn't a doctrine, it's a moral code, and if you haven't it, you just can't work it!

Those few words provide a compendium of her views on the world, and give a very fair indication of her strength and weakness.

9

Love Affair with Plymouth

&⳽⳾

NANCY'S relationship with Plymouth was not the ordinary relationship of an MP with his or her constituency. It was more that of a pastor, and still more that of a lover. She had an almost mystical sense of union with the place.

This began as we have seen, long before she was elected to represent the Sutton division. Her early letters to Phyllis show how much she loved being in Plymouth and how willingly she involved herself in the life of the people. But the feeling that she had in those early days never wore off. In 1935 she could still write to the Bishop of Plymouth: 'I don't feel I have had my holiday yet but it may come later. I'm looking forward to coming down to Plymouth again, because in a strange sort of way this always seems a holiday for me.'

Her conception of a special link between herself and Plymouth was intensified by her awareness of the historic link between Plymouth and the New World. Though it would have suited her better if the Pilgrim Fathers had sailed to Virginia, she nevertheless found a similarity between Virginians and Devonians, to which she referred when speaking in Plymouth after her visit to America in 1922:

I must tell you that my welcome in Virginia was best of all – Virginia, England's first child and my first home. All I can tell you is this: I got a Plymouth man a job in Virginia and I saw him when I got back home and he said: 'Lady Astor, you are right about Virginia. I didn't feel a bit away from Devon here. It's just like home.' And so I feel about Plymouth. It, too, to me is just like home. There's the same sort of naturalness about Virginians as there is about Devonians. We both have fine traditions, and perhaps we are both a little slow. The rest of the countries may pick out many faults in us, but they can also pick out many pages of history that would not have been written without us.

[155]

With ARP worker, during the Plymouth Blitz

Skating near Plymouth, 1933

There was nothing 'slow' about Nancy, and in her dealings with the people of Plymouth, which made her feel so close to them, she revelled in direct talk and lively backchat. Freddie Knox, who was brought up as a child in the Barbican and later became Nancy's devoted aide, stresses how different she was from other Conservative ladies – or gentlemen for that matter. 'She said: "We have got to get down to the people and if they don't know us we've got to get to know them." She came down right to the heart of the constituency and started going from door to door. She might well have been called the inventor of the walkabout.' According to Mr Knox, she used to say of the people that they were 'always so friendly but never familiar'. Whatever that may mean, they could be as direct with her as she was with them.

One night [Mr Knox says] we'd had a very rowdy meeting and they'd been firing questions and interruptions and hardly allowing her to speak. Next morning she came down and took a walk, which she liked to do, and they said to her: 'Good morning, my lady, how are you this morning?' 'How am I?' she said, 'How am I – after the roastin' you gave me last night? Why, you old devils, how do you think I am after all that?'

The recurrent phrase 'she came down' is significant, because although

Old friends' reunion: Waldorf with Queen Marie of Rumania on balcony of 3 Elliot Terrace, Plymouth, in the 1920s

Nancy *went* among the people when she was at Plymouth, she did not strictly *live* among them. The Hoe is a magnificent piece of high ground dominating both the harbour in front and the city behind. Number 3 Elliot Terrace was a modest house by comparison with 4 St James's Square, but it was and is one of the grandest houses in Plymouth. Acquiring it back in 1909, when Waldorf was only candidate for a difficult seat, was an act of faith on the Astors' part. In those days it was almost unheard-of for a local association to expect an MP from outside a constituency to acquire a residence in it, and the Plymouth Tories would never have expected the Astors to acquire one in Plymouth. When, however, they showed how much they wanted to be part of the place, there was a polite suggestion that they might buy a yacht, perhaps so that local worthies could be entertained on it. But Nancy stamped on this idea, saying: 'I've come to see the people, not to fish.'

Many royal and other important personages stayed at Elliot Terrace during

Nancy's twenty-five years as MP for the Sutton division, and most of them were 'taken down' to visit Virginia House or in some other way to meet 'the people'. Charlie Chaplin was one who came and his visit coincided with the annual blessing of the sea at Sutton harbour. Mrs Sleeman, daughter of one of Nancy's best friends in the harbour district, remembers the occasion well:

There were masses and masses of people, and Father phoned Lady Astor to say that she had to come down to the service. She said she would, and as she had Charlie Chaplin staying with her she brought him with her. The choirboys from St Andrew's Church changed into their surplices in our shop and the police had to make a pathway for them to the quayside. After the service the clergy and the choirboys came back across to the shop, followed by Lady Astor and Charlie Chaplin. Half way across he twisted his bowler-hat in the air, and of course the crowd went wild with delight.

By her combination of missionary zeal and vaudeville Nancy held the seat through six general elections. Her lowest majority was, predictably, in 1929 and her highest, no less predictably, in 1931, when for the only time it was in five figures and then only just. In 1929 she scraped in by only two hundred and eleven votes with the help, as we have seen, of Margaret McMillan. It is more than likely that any other candidate would have lost the seat in that year of Labour success.

During the 1929 election campaign she showed her mettle by taking the fight into the heart of enemy territory. How she got on was described by the *Daily Express* reporter who accompanied her:

'So you are a pack of Bolshies eh?'

Lady Astor stood with her feet squarely planted, a large umbrella clasped by the ferrule in her right hand, like a club, and her smart cloche hat at a rakish tilt.

She stood completely alone in the courtyard of the worst tenement of the worst street in Plymouth, a Communist stronghold, and glowered at balcony on balcony above her packed with more than a hundred shouting, shrieking, hostile women. 'So you are a pack of Bolshies eh?' she challenged, waving the umbrella threateningly.

'Better get away, Lady Astor,' I warned, for a hefty woman with sacking over her head was reaching for a cabbage.

She spun round fiercely. 'Leave this to me.' A man caught her roughly by the shoulder, and she raised the umbrella. He ran like a hare, and then she faced the crowd.

'Too proud for the working woman, am I?' She laughed merrily, and struck an attitude, nose perked comically, and danced affectedly up and down outside the tenement.

'They say I drink gin-and-bitters,' she cried. 'Hey, you up there.' She pointed to a woman who had been shouting herself hoarse. 'How many gin-and-bitters have I had with you, Pleasant?'

A little dog flew snarling at the crowd. Somebody threw a brick at him. Like an avenging angel with her umbrella, Lady Astor dashed up, saved the little dog, and then, with arms akimbo, harangued the crowd. Her words burned like acid.

[159]

Charlie Chaplin after the blessing of the sea ceremony, Sutton harbour

With a group of Plymouth women, May 1929

With members of Free Church Women's Council, Plymouth 1933

Such a fighting politician was in her element when the real war came. And it came with a vengeance to Plymouth. Together, she and Waldorf led the city through the worst experience in its history. In November 1939 Waldorf was elected Lord Mayor, thus becoming a successor to Drake who, though not normally associated with local government, was in fact Mayor of Plymouth in 1582. Waldorf was re-elected each year until 1944, and so served an unprecedented time in the office. As a result, Nancy was Lady Mayoress as well as MP for most of the war.

The first major Blitz on the city was during the night of 20–21 March 1941, after a visit by the King and Queen, whose train was leaving as the alert sounded. The city centre was hard hit and casualties were heavy, but it was only the beginning of a sustained onslaught that went on, with short intermissions, until the end of the year. During that first night an American writer, Ben Robertson, was staying with the Astors, and later wrote about it in a book entitled *I Saw England*:

At 8.30 p.m. we had eaten some chicken and stewed rhubarb and the cakes left over from the royal tea party, when . . . the guns began to thunder. From the very start there was

Waldorf and Nancy with George VI and Queen Elizabeth on the balcony of Elliot Terrace, within hours of the first Blitz on Plymouth

Nancy showing Dorothy Thompson, the famous American journalist, some of Plymouth's ruins, 1941

something about the intensity . . . which made us think this was it. We had all the tubs in the house filled with water and saw the spades were handy. . . . The air warden ordered Lady Astor to the basement. There she talked about Virginia and her childhood and the tobacco fields. . . . Someone came in to say that an incendiary was on the roof. 'Come on everybody,' called Lady Astor, 'get the sandbags. Where in hell are the buckets?' From this we were up and down the stairs. Once she stopped by a blasted window to look at Plymouth, which for miles was a blazing fire. Her eyes filled with tears and pushing back her steel hat she said: 'There goes thirty years of our lives, but we'll build it again.'

The rebuilding and re-planning of Plymouth was, in fact, Waldorf's greatest contribution. He persuaded his colleagues to invite Professor Patrick Abercrombie to do the job, and the necessary permissions were obtained. Abercrombie, who was then far less well-known than he later became, started work before the end of 1941. The plan that he drew up did much for his reputation, as it did for Plymouth.

Waldorf was not, however, with Nancy through most of the air raids, because in April he collapsed with what was described at the time as a chill, but is now considered by some to have been a mild stroke, by others a sort of nervous breakdown. Though he continued to attend to the affairs of the city, and to do so most effectively, it was Nancy who took most of the strain of actually being in Plymouth when it was under attack. A close relation, Alice Winn, who was with her during some of the worst of the bombing, gives this account of her on one day, which could go for many others:

Waldorf with a young Plymouth evacuee

[163]

We retired to bed and . . . all hell was let loose at ten o'clock. . . . The noise was deafening and the house rocked from side to side. No one appeared. The household was fatalistic. Ever since a motor car had been blown . . . on to the roof of the house they felt it quite useless to take precautions.

The next morning I got a message to hurry down as Lady Astor was waiting for me. She was smartly dressed as usual. . . . We motored to a badly bombed street in Devonport which was cordoned off. Piles of rubble and pools of water from broken water mains covered the street. Police, firemen and Red Cross people hurried about their business. We were told that the homeless were temporarily in a school hall. We walked there and on entering the large schoolroom we found the floor covered with mattresses on which exhausted people were stretched at full length. Children were restlessly climbing over their prostrate bodies. Down the middle of the hall was a passageway. Nannie advanced and said: 'Look here children, you can't do this.' So saying, clasping her umbrella and handbag tightly, she turned somersaults. [Not bad for a woman in her sixties.] This roused the children to screams of delight and their elders sat up and laughed. I heard them say, 'Well I never, look at Lady Astor!' . . . Nannie stood up neat and tidy as usual and merely said as she left the room, 'We are not downhearted, are we?' She knew that sympathy was not enough but laughter was healing.

When Winston Churchill and his wife visited Plymouth in May 1941, Nancy received them. She had recently started a national controversy by writing to *The Times* about the lack of any adequate system for fighting fires when big cities were attacked. In principle, she was right. Fire-fighting was still the responsibility of each local authority, which meant that in the exceptional circumstances of an incendiary raid the resources available to deal with fires were stretched far beyond the limit. As she toured Plymouth with Churchill he wept, and she said very audibly: 'It's all very well to cry, Winston, but you got to do somethin'.' Something was soon done. A National Fire Service was set up. This was not the solution that she herself had proposed, but it would almost certainly have been reached less swiftly if she had not raised the issue as and when she did.

Plymouth was not raided during 1942, but there were more severe attacks in 1943. By this time America was in the war, and American servicemen were stationed in the city. Their presence was very welcome to Nancy and she made them very welcome. Some American officers were put up by her at Elliot Terrace.

Another feature of wartime Plymouth, not actually initiated, but much encouraged by her, was dancing on the Hoe. She would climb over the railings outside her house, pick up a sailor, dance a round with him, pick up a soldier and so on. As always, her liveliness and sheer star quality did much to make the party go.

Her marvellous work in Plymouth prompts the question: Should she not have been given a larger role during the war? When Churchill was forming his Government he offered a junior post to Waldorf, Parliamentary Secretary to the

Community dancing on the Hoe: the Lord and Lady Mayoress step out

Ministry of Agriculture, but for various reasons Waldorf turned it down. No ministerial post was at any time offered to Nancy, however, and there is no evidence that the idea of offering her one was even considered. Was this right?

Apart from Churchill's prejudice against her (which her dig at him when they were touring Plymouth together can have done nothing to remove), there were plenty of arguments that could have been used against making her a minister. She had never run anything except her own (admittedly large) houses, and the ways of Whitehall were very far from being hers. She hated bureaucracy and was particularly scathing in her attacks on local officialdom for what she regarded as its rigidity and lack of imagination during the Blitz. She was clearly, too, by nature very indiscreet, tending to speak first and think afterwards. Moreover, she was very partisan, and her hostility to the Labour Party grew rather than diminished during the war, while Labour ministers were serving in Churchill's coalition and there was, supposedly, a party truce. Beyond question it would have been difficult for even a prime minister who favoured her to fit her into his team.

On the other hand, there is a case to be made for Nancy. Even in normal times it is too easily taken for granted that a minister has to be a good administrator. But is that really an indispensable qualification? Ministers have the backing of ministries, whose function it is to see that rules are enforced and decisions carried out. Ministers do not have to be machines, because they have a machine at their disposal. Their task is to drive the machine and to make sure that it moves in the right direction. Surely, therefore, it is more important for them to be *animators* than administrators; and if that is true in normal times, how much more so in the abnormal conditions of war.

Nancy was an animator if ever there was one. She had the sort of intuitions that bureaucrats seldom have, and to some extent are trained not to have. In her political life she often had the flair to perceive that something was worth doing, but she then depended upon the staffwork of others, especially Waldorf, to get it done. She provided both the animating spark and the dynamism to keep the enterprise in motion. She also had the theatrical gifts that are needed for almost any large-scale enterprise, whether public or private.

Since she was able to achieve quite a lot as a back-bench MP, with the help of Waldorf and her secretaries (about five of them), might she not have achieved a good deal more with the help of a government department? In war-time people could have been expected to make allowances for any lack of ministerial decorum: many would surely have welcomed it. And if her methods had been somewhat irregular, they could hardly have been more so than Beaverbrook's or, for that matter, Churchill's.

As, say, junior minister for Home Security she might have given the whole country the benefit of those qualities for which Plymouth had such good reason to be thankful. It seems a pity that she was not tried in that post, or in some other with a comparable bearing upon civilian morale. There are many examples of politicians who have been condemned as irresponsible until entrusted with responsibility. Nancy might have been a case in point, but unfortunately she was denied the chance to prove herself, one way or the other.

Left a freelance, she certainly did seem rather irresponsible at times – as, for instance, when she attacked the Russians at a United Nations rally. She did herself no good when, in 1943, she was caught obtaining clothes, illegally, through a friend in the American Red Cross, and was fined fifty pounds with costs at Bow Street. In general, and despite her heroism at Plymouth, her reputation sagged as the war went on.

It was not all her own fault. The Cliveden Set myth continued to harm her, and there were ugly rumours against her in the armed forces. She was said to have tried to stop a system of special payments to sailors called 'hard-lying money' (an allowance to compensate sailors working under particularly difficult conditions) of which, in fact, she had never heard. She was accused of having talked of the Eighth Army basking in the sun while people at home were being bombed. There was a rumour that she had said all men coming back from the Middle East should wear yellow arm-bands as a warning against VD, and another – which circulated in prison camps – that she had said English girls would not marry Englishmen because they were cowards, but were marrying men from the Dominions instead. All these charges she hotly denied.

In December 1944 she received a letter from a private in the Buffs regiment, serving in Italy, which was signed 'D-Day Dodgers'. She, assuming this was a humorous nickname like 'Desert Rats', began her reply 'Dear D-Day Dodgers', only to find that it was soon being put around she had cast an odious slur on the army in Italy. This and some of the other rumours may have been due in the first place to honest misunderstanding, but Nancy was convinced that they were part of a deliberate and politically-motivated campaign of character assassination.

Above all, the spirit of the times was against her. The war marked a decisive change in public attitudes and public policy – a change towards the collectivism that Waldorf rather liked but Nancy hated. She was a social reformer who felt that society should be improved largely on private initiative, with the State helping but not taking over. The new emphasis upon State action supplanting private charity offended her deepest instincts.

The changing mood was evident in Plymouth, though she seems not to have noticed it. Even before the war there was always an undercurrent of hostility to the Astor regime. Local Labourites not unnaturally felt that they were having to fight Santa Claus, which added a sense of injustice to their belief that tinkering with social evils, however well-intentioned, was no answer to the social problem.

During the war this feeling became more widespread. While Nancy's courage and leadership were admired, her political style began to cause rather more annoyance than in the past. Noël Coward was a shrewd observer who visited Plymouth in 1941 to ensure accuracy of detail for his film, *In Which We Serve*. His impressions of the city and of Nancy at the time are quoted in Cole Lesley's life of him:

Drove to Grand Hotel through terrible devastation. A heart-breaking sight. Had drinks at hotel with Dorothy the barmaid. She told me stories of the blitzes here, quite without conscious drama, therefore infinitely more touching. It certainly is a pretty exciting thing to be English. Spent next morning with Lady Astor walking round the devastated town. A strange experience. Lady Astor very breezy, noisy and *au fond* incredibly kind, banging people on the back and making jokes. The people themselves stoic, sometimes resentful of her, but generally affectionately tolerant. . . . [At lunch] Lady A delivered tirade against

Winston. Also said apropos of Bruce Lockhart that he could not be a really good appointment [he had just been made director of political warfare at the Foreign Office] because he had written a book discussing his travels in Europe with his mistress. This point of view baffling and irritating. How sad that a woman of such kindness and courage should be a fanatic.

The picture is of an MP still loved, if only in a 'tolerant' way, by most of her constituents, but also of some antagonism towards her. Later in the war this antagonism had become more pronounced, and the tolerance less so. Among local Conservatives there was a strong feeling that she ought not to stand again at the next election, though few would have dared to say this to her.

The decision was taken out of their hands – by Waldorf. He was at loggerheads with the Plymouth Conservatives himself, because many of them were opposed to his plan for the city, which conflicted with some private interests. Though he would have liked to be re-elected for a fifth term as Lord Mayor, the Conservative group in the council in effect pushed him out, because they felt that the time had come for a resumption of party politics. (He had been elected unopposed, and served throughout in a non-partisan spirit.)

Nobody could accuse Nancy of being insufficiently partisan, but it was feared that her brand of electioneering might seem anachronistic in the new climate. There was also a view, which Waldorf shared, that her judgment was not what it used to be, and that she would damage her credit by remaining in politics. Moreover, Waldorf felt that his health would not be equal to another general

With Michael (left) and Jakie (right), during the Second World War

[168]

election campaign, and it was generally assumed that she would not be able to fight without his help and support.

When, therefore, *he* wrote to the Conservative Association to say that she would not be standing, the decision was accepted with only one dissentient. Nobody seems to have thought it necessary – or prudent – to check with her that she really wanted to withdraw. The one who dissented was Freddie Knox. He now makes this comment on how the decision was taken: 'Several of them knew that she wanted to stand, and lots of them, I think, sheltered behind Lord Astor in allowing him to say what, perhaps, they felt but didn't dare to say to her.'

The announcement that she would not be standing again was made on 1 December 1944, the twenty-fifth anniversary of her entry into the House of Commons. At a celebratory dinner that evening she said: 'I have said that I will not fight the next election because my husband does not want me to. . . . Isn't that a triumph for the men?' It was not in her nature to pretend that the decision was hers or that she liked it.

In 1945, therefore, her political career came to an end, and at the same time she and Waldorf ended their long period of joint service to Plymouth. Together they had done great things for the city, and she, as the first woman to sit in Parliament, had added new lustre to its history. But as yet the city has shown little sign that it is proud of the Astors' achievements or that it appreciates what they did.

Waldorf was made a Freeman in 1936, but this honour was not conferred upon Nancy until 1959, after her eightieth birthday. Even then it was conferred only by a vote of the Conservative majority, and when she came to receive it most Labour members of the council boycotted the ceremony.

Most visible memorials to the Astors in Plymouth were presented by themselves. Apart from the institutions that they had already endowed, Elliot Terrace was bequeathed as a residence for future lord mayors – though in fact it is only used now and then for civic hospitality – and Nancy gave a diamond necklace to be worn by future lady mayoresses.

Some years ago an attempt was made to have Guildhall Square renamed Waldorf Astor Square or Astor Square, but the Labour Party objected. Less understandably, suggestions that a statue should be put up in some public place have come to nothing. There is an Astor Room, containing a bust of Nancy, inside the Guildhall, but no monument out in the open, where citizens and visitors to the city could see it – and be reminded. A statue on the Hoe would, surely, be the right solution.

Her own idea of a memorial to herself in Plymouth was more prosaic. She used to say that she would like the city to be covered with litter bins to keep it clean and tidy.

10

Long Farewell

LEAVING politics was a terrible blow to Nancy. She was never reconciled
to it nor did she ever forgive Waldorf for doing to her what, she believed,
the electors of Sutton would not have done. She was sure that, if she had
stood in 1945, she would have held the seat. As usual, Waldorf acted in what he
imagined to be her best interests, but in that he may have been mistaken. He
certainly acted very much against his own.

David Astor has this to say of the decision that clouded his parents' last years
together:

[He] thought that she really had rather lost her grip on current politics. He consulted a
whole lot of her political friends and they all, without exception, said she shouldn't go on.
But when Mother put it to them they all flattered her and said, 'You're as good as you ever
were.' My father never told me this. He took the odium entirely on himself and it
did cause a very unpleasant relationship for quite a while. My mother really felt that she
had been deprived of her life, and my father felt he had no choice in her interest. Had he
been a more cynical man he would have said 'Well go on, stand, and see what happens.'
But he couldn't have done that. My father would have died for my mother any day of the
week, and he just wasn't able to do that.

If he had done the 'cynical' thing, it is likely, though it cannot be certain, that
Nancy would have been beaten. With a new candidate, Colonel Grand, the
Conservatives lost to the Labour candidate, Mrs Middleton, by a majority of over
4,500, and the seat was not recaptured until the 1951 election, when it was won
by Nancy's son, Jakie. It had never been a safe seat. As we have seen, Nancy very
nearly lost it in 1929, and it is hard to believe that even she could have held it
against the much stronger Labour tide of 1945.

But, from her point of view as well as Waldorf's, might it not have been better
if she had tried to hold it? The idea that defeat would have broken her heart surely
does her less than justice. She was a very tough character who could still, at sixty-
six, take what was coming to her. If she had fought and lost she would have been
spared the misery of feeling that her absence from the new Parliament was

Nancy on her eightieth birthday

Waldorf in old age, in the hall at Cliveden

unnecessary, and her next-of-kin would have been spared the flail of her reproaches.

The State did nothing to dignify the moment of her departure from politics. In 1937 she had been made a Companion of Honour, but eight years later, despite all that she had done in Plymouth during the war, she received no further award. It would have been for Churchill to recommend her for some honour, but his prejudice must have blinded him to the obvious fitness of a gesture to her of this kind at the end of her trail-blazing stint in Parliament. And he was guilty of an even worse sin of omission the following year, when he addressed the Virginian Legislature. In a fine peroration on the many historic links between Virginia and England, he never so much as mentioned Nancy. This astonished many of those present and seems no less astonishing in retrospect.

Deprived simultaneously of two spheres of activity that had meant so much to her, the House of Commons and Plymouth, Nancy lost interest in public work. She did not take up any cause or launch any charitable enterprise, but spent the last nineteen years of her life doing nothing in particular. Waldorf approached various committees in whose work he thought she might be interested, but found that they were reluctant to have her as a member. The idea, anyway, was misconceived, because she was not made to be a committee woman.

Waldorf needed her support. His heart was weak and he suffered increasingly from asthma. But Nancy could give him little sympathy. Having been emancipated from nervous illness by Christian Science, and having a basically rock-like constitution, she could not understand organic weakness or the troubles to which it gave rise. Besides, she was furious with Waldorf, and her resentment choked the compassion that she should have felt for him.

St James's Square was sold, but another London house was bought for her – 35 Hill Street, in Mayfair. She spent most of her time there, or at Sandwich, or travelling, while Waldorf spent the rest of his life largely at Cliveden, though with interludes at David's country house at Sutton Courtenay. There were times when Nancy and Waldorf were together at Cliveden, but only in the sense that they were under the same roof. It was not until he was near to dying that she relented.

They might have been reconciled sooner – indeed, the estrangement might never have occurred – if Philip Lothian had been alive. But he had died in December 1940, at the height of his powers, while serving as British Ambassador in the United States. He was a martyr to Christian Science, because his illness, uraemia, could have been treated, and his life prolonged, if he had not refused medical assistance. Nancy heard the news of his death at Plymouth, and according to Rose Harrison it was one of the rare occasions when she broke down and wept.

In the last phase of his life she was no longer his only confidante. Though she did not know it, he was in close correspondence with Ava Wigram, later Ava Waverley, a woman more intellectual than Nancy, and with a mind that could match the Jesuitical intricacy of his own. All the same, he remained deeply attached to the Astors, and his influence might well have averted the disastrous quarrel over Nancy's political future.

Bernard Shaw was too old to want her company any more. After his wife's death in 1943 he only asked to be left alone, and although he was still very fond of Nancy he found even brief visits from her rather a strain. When she proposed that he should live with her in London, he refused point-blank, saying that he hated London and did not wish to leave his familiar surroundings at Ayot St Lawrence. But when she then threatened to move in with him there, he replied that nothing would more swiftly persuade him to move to London. She was joking, of course, and so was he, but only because he knew that she did not mean it.

The lodger she did have at Hill Street was her brother-in-law, Bob Brand, and he has left a good description of her in that setting:

[173]

I always looked in at her in her bedroom before I went to my office in the morning. She has breakfast early and then surrounds herself with Christian Science books all over her bed and fits the little markers into all the texts in the Old and New Testaments ordained by the Christian Science authorities for the week. . . . When I go in to see her, however, it is much more than fifty to one that she is telephoning. It is at this hour that like a commander-in-chief she gives to numerous relations and friends their instructions or invitations for the day. So how much of a look-in Mrs Eddy's books really got I never knew.

All her Astor sons were married, and her attitude towards their wives was predictably uncordial. The one she came to like best was, ironically, the Roman Catholic, Chiquita, who has given this most vivid physical account of her:

Her eyes are very pale blue and sharp even when they are distorted by laughter. Her gaze has the power of going through walls and souls. . . . She often wears blue to match her eyes. This is her favourite colour. She always has a gentle scarf loosely round her neck and it ranges from a pale to a rich azure. The scarf is pinned with a brooch holding a sprig of sweet-smelling geranium, and this I shall always identify with her as she never wears scent.

She loves food, jewellery, china and human beings, also cold water, fresh air and exercise. I have often watched her practise golf . . . and noticed how short her arms and legs are. These are so strong and agile that they remind me of a Chinese wrestler's legs. The feet are small and strong like the hands, with very short fingers that have a magical touch when it comes to rubbing one's head.

Late in 1950 Waldorf had a stroke. Thereafter she spent more time with him and something of their old intimacy was restored. On 30 September 1952 he died, and soon afterwards she wrote to Tom Jones (who had annoyed her by backing Waldorf on the issue of her leaving Parliament):

You need not tell me how fond you were of Waldorf. . . . My only regret is that he was ever influenced by you!! . . . We had forty happy years together. No two people ever worked happier than we did, . . . thank God he was like his old self the last ten days and oh how it makes me grieve of the years wasted! . . . But I don't want to look back but forward.

Clearly she was very sorry, but not penitent. Waldorf left a great void in her life, but the nearest she could come to forgiving him was to blame a friend for misleading him.

The irony of it was that *she* had destroyed *his* career, rather than vice versa. If either had cause for complaint on that score, it was Waldorf. The mere inheritance of a peerage would not necessarily have debarred him from high office – might even have helped him, because the competition is less hot in the House of Lords – but devoting himself as he did to her career put him effectively out of the running. He could hardly have expected to reach the very highest places in any case, but if

[175]

A late picture of Waldorf and Nancy together

his wife had not been Nancy it is quite possible, even likely, that he would have become a Cabinet minister.

Though, at first, he may have hoped that her tenure of the Sutton division would be short, and that he would soon be free to resume it, once he saw that she was in the House of Commons to stay, he concentrated upon doing all that he could to help her make a success of her political role. To that extent he willingly sacrificed his prospects to hers. His life was in many ways fruitful, and may be cited as a strong argument in favour of inherited wealth, but unquestionably the pattern of his life's work was distorted for her sake.

Together they were a great partnership, and Nancy would have been almost lost in politics without him, after his health collapsed. It was sad that she did not repay his unselfishness in kind during the last years of their marriage.

The year after he died, when she was on her annual visit to the United States (which in 1953 was longer than usual), she met Senator Joseph MacCarthy at a party. She asked him what he was drinking, and when he replied that it was whisky, she said, 'I wish it was poison.' This was an echo of a famous exchange with Churchill many years before, when she had said that if she were his wife she would put poison in his coffee, and he had retorted that if he were married to her he would drink it.

In the summer of 1953 she was travelling again, this time to Rhodesia. The country attracted her as an African version, she thought, of Virginia, and her trip there was a success. One of those who entertained her was the Chief Justice, Sir Robert Tredgold, who has written in his memoirs, *The Rhodesia That Was My Life*:

[Nancy] was asked to meet a group of African intellectuals . . . . I think they expected a sentimental liberal and were taken aback by her frankness and realism, yet, by the end of the evening, they were completely captivated. We talked with freedom on all the subjects normally gingerly avoided in inter-racial discussion, even down to intermarriage. She took them aback, again, by expressing herself firmly against this, but then proceeded to give her reasons in a manner that removed any possible cause of offence. . . . One answer stuck in my mind. She was asked by an aggressive nationalist whether she thought her son better than his, and retorted: 'Which son are you talking about? I have five. One I would trust to run the Empire. Another I wouldn't trust to take me across Berkeley Square.'

If by the other she meant Bobbie, he was nevertheless still the closest of all to her. But as she entered her last decade the ferocious banter which for so long had been the stock-in-trade between them began to hurt her more than it hurt him, whereas in the past it had probably been the other way round. Her memory was failing and her mind was losing its quickness, though still capable of brilliant flashes. Verbal counter-attack was becoming more of an effort to her, and one day

Nancy with two of her grandchildren, William and Emily Astor

at Sandwich she was so exasperated by Bobbie's goading that she picked up a jug of white wine cup and emptied it over his head, to the bewilderment of two strangers who had been asked to lunch.

A new friend in her widowhood was Judy Musters, a cousin of Bernard Shaw (who had died in 1950). Mrs Musters, also a widow, helped Nancy to come to terms with old age, though her proposal that occupational therapy should be sought in the form of a new crusade went unheeded.

Another special friend of Nancy's last phase was Freda Casa Maury, formerly, as Freda Dudley Ward, the Duke of Windsor's steadiest love before Mrs Simpson. She had long been a friend of Bobbie, but had hardly known Nancy until, in the war, she had to visit her husband who was stationed in Plymouth. There she was recognized by Nancy in the street, and asked to make Elliot Terrace her home for all future visits. The only condition was that she must be acceptable to the staff. (NA: 'Are you all right with servants?' FCM: 'Oh yes, I always do exactly what they tell me.' NA: 'Very well, but if I have any complaints you will be out in the street at once.') Marquesa Casa Maury remembers walking one morning in the neighbourhood of Hill Street and being stopped in her tracks by the noise of laughter and backchat coming, as it seemed, from under the ground. Soon the cause was revealed to her, as Nancy emerged from an open drain, where her presence had been a surprising, but welcome, distraction to the workmen.

In 1958 she sold Hill Street and took a large flat at 100 Eaton Square, which ran the length of four converted houses. This was her last London address. By now she was seeing fewer people, partly for the sad reason that fewer people wanted to visit her. Unlike her father she had always tended to repeat her stories, and with advancing years the 'gramophone record' became more pronounced. Yet she could still put on a marvellous show, as she did when interviewed by Kenneth Harris for BBC Television on the occasion of her eightieth birthday.

At this time women were being appointed to life peerages, an innovation brought in by Harold Macmillan, whom she had befriended as a young politician. Though she had no idea of returning to active Parliamentary work, it would have pleased her very much to be among the first women to sit in the 'other place', having been the first to sit in the House of Commons, and she was, therefore, very hurt that Mr Macmillan did not recommend her for a life peerage. Indeed, it does seem most unfortunate that this recognition was denied her.

Her body failed more slowly than her mind. Until a late stage she continued to swim and play golf. In the old days, when she went swimming at Sandwich, Waldorf would insist that she tie a rope round her waist, and he would then sit on the beach, holding the end of the rope (a perfect symbol of their relationship). Without such a safety precaution it was a serious risk for a woman nearing her eighties to expose herself to the Channel waves, and gradually she was persuaded

The relentless tennis player

[179]

to give up sea-bathing, which she had always particularly loved. On her eightieth birthday she could still swing a golf club convincingly, but actually playing her favourite game was becoming impossible for her.

It was necessary, but not easy, to stop her driving a car. She had always been a solipsistic driver, and had been lucky not to kill herself or others. Alice Winn remembers returning once from the Christian Science church in Maidenhead, with Nancy driving on the wrong side of the road. They met a policeman who held up his hand to stop her, but she drove on twenty yards or so before stopping. When he asked 'Didn't you see my hand was up?' she replied disarmingly 'If you'd known who was driving you'd have put up both your hands'. Many such stories are told of her until quite late on, but finally she resigned herself to being always driven.

More remarkable was her acquiescence in having medical attention when she was ill. Shortly before she was eighty she had a quinsy in her throat which prevented her eating and so made her alarmingly thin. Rose Harrison was so worried that she telephoned David and begged him to help. By putting it to her that she ought to think of her family if not of herself, he managed somehow to persuade her to see a doctor. Thereafter she accepted the need for medical help in certain eventualities.

She also allowed herself to be conned (perhaps) into drinking Dubonnet as a substitute for Ribena, and even graduated to drinking the occasional egg-nog, which had been one of her father's special mixtures. All witnesses are agreed that her religious dogmatism and austerity gave way to something akin to mellowness in her very last years. She became, too, so indiscriminately generous with her money that her cheque-book had to be removed.

Her more relaxed attitude towards the rules of Christian Science did not betoken any loss of religious feeling or aspiration. She remained an American girl in search of God. After the war she became acquainted with a young Episcopal clergyman, the Revd Douglas Pitt, who had worked with her old friend, Archdeacon Neve. He was thus a link with Virginia, to which her mind was increasingly reverting, and she liked to correspond with him on spiritual matters – all the more so, perhaps, as she may have felt that he, like herself, was not entirely indifferent to the world's charm. Mr Pitt speaks of her amusingly, affectionately and with wisdom. He feels that her Christian Science was superimposed upon the Episcopalianism of her childhood, but never completely replaced it. One of the attractions to her of Christian Science, he feels, was that in its Wednesday night services it provided scope for audience participation. 'It gave her a chance to get up and speak in church, which she couldn't do in the Anglican church in those days.' In his view, she was 'always striving for something in religion that she never quite achieved'. She once said to him: 'When I read my Christian Science lesson in the morning I feel I can go out and raise the dead. But what happens? I go out and raise the devil.'

When Waldorf died, Bill inherited the tenancy of Cliveden. He could not be the owner, because in 1942 Waldorf had made the estate over to the National Trust. Nancy went back there occasionally, but not very often, and when she did she gave Bill the feeling that his changes and improvements were not at all congenial to her. Probably the happiest visit was for a family party there in honour of her eightieth birthday. But on the whole she preferred staying with her niece, Nancy Lancaster, at Great Haseley in Oxfordshire, or with her daughter, Wissie, at Grimsthorpe in Lincolnshire. Wissie, who in the past had been terrified of her mother, was now able to control her.

In 1963 Cliveden came into the news far more sensationally than in the pre-war period, and the idea of a 'Cliveden Set' acquired a new meaning. The model whom Michael had brought there as a young man turned out to be the first swallow in what, later, was an over-luxuriant summer. One girl in particular became a household name on account of her affair with a senior Conservative minister, who had first seen her, naked, in the Cliveden swimming pool, itself one of Bill's innovations. (Nancy used to swim in the river.)

The Profumo scandal provided good copy for the lubricious, prying journalism that became fashionable in the Sixties, and one of its effects was to bring upon Bill an odium that was partly moral, partly social. The girl in the case was one of a number who had been introduced to the Cliveden scene by Bill's osteopath, Stephen Ward, who had a house on the estate. And there is a terrible irony, which the ancient Greeks would have appreciated, in the fact that Ward was introduced to Bill by Bobbie Shaw.

Ward, a deeply unpleasant man who despised the women he exploited (socially, if not financially), because he had a resentful contempt for women in general, became almost a cult figure of the 'permissive society' when he committed suicide to escape conviction on charges of immorality. At the same time Bill, a kindly man, if weak, was savagely condemned in the same quarters for his alleged failure to support Ward at his trial. Few bothered to consider that if the defence had thought Bill's evidence on oath would be helpful to their cause he would certainly have been subpoenaed. In any case, he had offered to testify.

There was desperate, possibly excessive, anxiety in the family as to the effect the scandal might have upon Nancy, and for a time she was kept in ignorance of it by various subterfuges. Stories about it in the newspapers would be cut out before the papers were given to her and friends would be mobilized to telephone her just before the news bulletins at one o'clock and six. If she had been anything like her old self these tricks would of course never have worked. As it was she found out eventually and then merely asked to be taken to see Bill. There was no sign that

Grimsthorpe Castle, Lincolnshire: the old front

either her health or her heart was broken.

Very different was her reaction when, the following year, Bobbie tried to kill himself by taking an overdose of sleeping pills. Nancy was in the South of France at the time with Wissie, who at first kept the news from her mother. But soon her brothers dissuaded her from this course. She then told Nancy that Bobbie had had a stroke and brought her back to England.

Nancy visited him in St Stephen's Hospital, which was near his house off the Fulham Road. Probably she guessed, or felt instinctively, what had really happened. At any rate Wissie and Nancy Lancaster noticed a change in her when she came back from the hospital. It may be that she had had a slight stroke, brought on by an intuition that her favourite son no longer wished to live. And his suicidal frame of mind was, no doubt, largely due to his awareness that she was slipping away from him. A few days later she went to stay with Wissie and her husband, James Ancaster, at their Lincolnshire home, Grimsthorpe – a magnificent place, partly built by Vanbrugh. On arrival she had what was unmistakably a stroke, and was put to bed in the old, south side of the house. The date was 18 April 1964.

Soon it became clear that she was dying. A doctor attended her, and she did not object. To him she said, one day, that considering she was dying she felt very well. Nurses came to look after her, and she did not object to them either. One night nurse, who was a keen golfer, was surprised to be asked by her patient, then very near the end, to demonstrate her swing. She did so and Nancy murmured 'Not bad'.

[182]

OPPOSITE *Old, but still elegant*

Relations came to see her, knowing it would be for the last time. David had the impression that her mind was far away, probably in Virginia. Michael, too, felt that she was back in her childhood, taking him for one of her brothers. But she also called out for Waldorf.

Jakie gives this moving account of his last visit to her:

She was lying back, with her very beautiful, well-structured face. She was very peaceful, her eyes closed. I sat beside her for a bit and then she opened her eyes and saw I was there. She looked me straight in the face and said 'Jakie, is it my birthday or am I dying?' – which was quite a difficult one to answer. So I said 'A bit of both, Mum', and then she closed her eyes. I never saw her again.

In all his dealings with her he had never been at a loss for an answer. Years before, when he and Waldorf were driving off to the races, Nancy had shouted through the window 'Don't forget, racin' brings out the worst in all classes', and he had replied 'Just like the House of Commons'. It was right that his last remark to her should be a flight of wit touching the sublime.

Her character was strong and wilful to the end. Indeed she hastened the end by clenching her teeth and refusing food and drink. In a sense she killed herself, knowing that she could not recover. Had she let nature take its course she might have lived to her eighty-fifth birthday, instead of dying barely a fortnight short of it, in the early morning of 2 May 1964. Her adventure, which had begun in a one-storeyed wooden house in Danville, Virginia, ended in one of the stateliest of England's stately homes.

Her ashes were buried with Waldorf's in the eighteenth-century Octagon Temple at Cliveden, just below the great lawn (on which she used to practise golf shots) and near the Canadian war cemetery. A Confederate flag, given to her in Danville in 1922, was buried with her. In mid-May there was a conspicuously well-attended memorial service to her in Westminster Abbey.

Bill did not long survive her. He died, a broken-spirited man, in 1966, and after his death the Astor connection with Cliveden came to an end. Bobbie lived on, unexpectedly, until 1970, when he took a successful overdose. Life without Nancy was hateful to him, and his agony of spirit was often pitiable, though it could take a brutal form. He and Bill are both buried in the Octagon Temple; Bill in a straight line from his parents and paternal grandfather; Bobbie slightly to one side, even in death apparently the odd man out.

As at Plymouth, so in London, there is no outdoor memorial to Nancy. A statue of Mrs Pankhurst stands in Victoria Gardens, near the Palace of Westminster, but there is no statue of Nancy there or anywhere else in London. Even in the House of Commons the only memorial is a photograph (apart from a bust of her in the Speaker's house). The large picture by Charles Sims, showing her with Lloyd George and Balfour before her introduction, was rejected by MPs when Waldorf presented it in 1924, and now lies in a storehouse at the university of Virginia, Charlottesville.

One day she will be properly commemorated in the building that she gatecrashed on behalf of her sex; also, one hopes, in one of London's more public places. She may not have had an original mind, but her personality was brilliant and, in more than the trite sense, unique. Above all, she had the spirit of a pioneer, and so was able to accomplish, undaunted, her historic pioneering mission.

The Octagon Temple at Cliveden

HERE REST THE MINGLED ASHES OF
WALDORF 2ND VISCOUNT ASTOR
AND NANCY VISCOUNTESS ASTOR C.H
BORN MAY 19TH 1879
DIED SEPTEMBER 30TH 1952 AND
MAY 2ND 1964

Grave of Waldorf and Nancy

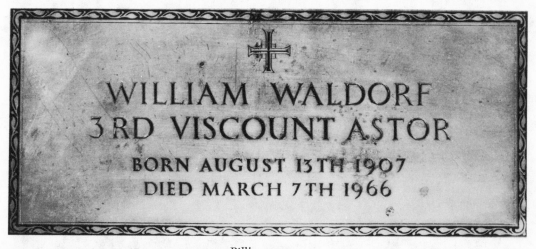

WILLIAM WALDORF
3RD VISCOUNT ASTOR
BORN AUGUST 13TH 1907
DIED MARCH 7TH 1966

Bill's grave

ROBERT GOULD SHAW
BORN AUGUST 18TH 1898
DIED JULY 10TH 1970

Bobbie's grave

Note on Sources

The main primary source on Nancy and Waldorf is the Astor archive in the Library of Reading University. This is massive and in excellent order. It includes the autobiographical fragment that Nancy wrote – or had ghost-written for her – after her retirement from politics.

The most important privately-held documents used in the book are the letters written by Nancy to her sister Phyllis before the First World War. They belong to Phyllis's elder daughter, the Hon. Lady Ford.

The Cliveden visitors' books, covering the whole period of Nancy's association with the place, are of great value as evidence of who did and did not go there, of who was there with whom, and of when particular people were there. The books are Viscount Astor's property.

The author has had the benefit of research and interviews conducted for a BBC2 television documentary on Nancy, of which he was the presenter. He has also been allowed to quote from essays on Nancy written some years ago, at Michael Astor's request, by a variety of people who knew her well.

Among printed sources special value attaches to Michael Astor's book of personal and family reminiscence, *Tribal Feeling*; to Alice Winn's *Always a Virginian* (published, unfortunately, only in America); and to Rosina Harrison's *Rose: My Life in Service*. All three give vivid, first-hand accounts of Nancy, as do Joyce Grenfell's *Joyce Grenfell Requests the Pleasure* and *In Pleasant Places*.

By far the best biography is Christopher Sykes's *Nancy: The Life of Lady Astor*, a masterly work showing none of the hostile bias that might have been expected from a Roman Catholic writer dealing with someone so strongly prejudiced against his faith. Other biographies containing useful information are Maurice Collis's *Nancy Astor: An Informal Biography* and Elizabeth Langhorne's *Nancy Astor and Her Friends*.

On the Astor dynasty in general the most up-to-date book is *The Astors: the Story of a Transatlantic Family* by Virginia Cowles. On the political background to

Nancy's career as a woman MP, *Women in Westminster* by Pamela Brookes is most useful.

As well as Hansard and the Press, other published sources on which the author has drawn are diaries, memoirs and biographies of Nancy's friends and contemporaries. He has also been helped by personal knowledge and much private information.

Index

(Figures in italics refer to illustrations)

Index